GOING TOP SHELF

GOING TOP SHELF
An Anthology of Canadian Hockey Poetry

Edited by
Michael P.J. Kennedy

VICTORIA · VANCOUVER · CALGARY

Heritage House Publishing Company Ltd.
heritagehouse.ca

Library and Archives Canada Cataloguing in Publication

Going top shelf : an anthology of Canadian hockey poetry / Michael
P. J. Kennedy, editor.

ISBN 1-894384-99-7

1. Canadian poetry (English)--20th century. 2. Hockey—Poetry.
I. Kennedy, Michael P. J.

PS8287.H63G64 2005   C811'.54080357   C2005-904039-4

Edited by Corina Skavberg
Book design by One Below
Cover design by One Below
Front cover photo Glenbow Archives ND-3-6985ggg

Heritage House acknowledges the financial support for its publishing program from the Government of Canada through the Canada Book Fund (CBF), Canada Council for the Arts and the Province of British Columbia through the British Columbia Arts Council and the Book Publishing Tax Credit.

17 16 15   3 4 5

Printed and bound in Canada

Acknowledgements

Many thanks to my wife Marjorie Kennedy for her continued support of all my teaching, research, writing, and community endeavours. Sincere thanks to each author for providing the excellent poems and song lyrics which have made this book possible, and to my niece, Shauna May, for her insights into contemporary Canadian music. Gratitude is also expressed to University of Saskatchewan Huskie Men's Hockey Programme for all its assistance. Special thanks to our game, hockey, for providing the common vehicle used in such unique ways by so many creative artists throughout this anthology.

"Me Like Hockey" lyrics appear through the courtesy of The Arrogant Worms and Michael McCormick.

The Porcupine's Quill Inc. has granted permission for publication of "Thaw" by Margaret Avison which appeared in *Always Now: The Collected Poems of Margaret Avison*, Erin, Ontario, Porcupine's Quill, 2003.

"In The Hockey Hall of Fame I Sat Down and Wept" is used here by permission of the author, Roger Bell.

"At The Arena" by Kelley Jo Burke appears by permission of the author.

Barry Butson's "Classic City Arena on Friday Nights" appears by permission of the author.

Nils Clausson's "Breakaway Sonnet" is published here by permission of the author.

Lyrics to "The Hockey Song" are supplied with permission by the author, Stompin' Tom Connors, Morning Music Limited and Crown Vetch Music.

Lorna Crozier's "Canadian Angels" first appeared on CBC Radio in 2001. It appears here thanks to the author's approval.

The lyrics to "Hockey Skates" by Kathleen Edwards appear through the courtesy of the author and Egg Plant Entertainment.

"Rink" and "Grey is the Forelock Now of the Irishman" are published here with the permission of the author Joan Finnigan.

"New Skates" and "Dragging Buses with Your Teeth" by C.H. (Marty) Gervais are published here by permission of the author.

Don Gutteridge's "Arena" reprinted from *A True History of Lambton County*, appears here thanks to the author and Oberon Press in Ottawa.

"Coach's Corner," "Rheaume," "Defence Mechanisms," "Fogarty," and "What It Takes" by Richard Harrison are republished here by permission of the author and Wolsak and Wynn of Toronto.

Gerry Hill's "Anecdote of the Hockey Game" is published with the permission of the author.

Gary Hyland's "The B-P-T" appears through the courtesy of the author.

Donna Kane's "Summer Hockey Camp" is published with the permission of the author.

Michael P.J. Kennedy's "I Am Hockey" appears by permission of the author.

"The Hockey Player Sonnets," "My Father Quit Hockey One Night Late in His Youth," "Dying on the Ice at Age 39," "Christmas Hockey Game, Faculty versus Students," "The Hockey Player Sonnets" and "When I was a Boy and the Family Pond Froze" all appear by permission of the author, John B. Lee, and Penumbra Press.

Hugh MacDonald's "Behind the Red Brick House: Charlottetown, P.E.I. 1955" appears with the permission of the author.

Florence McNeil's "Family Pond" is published here through the permission of the author.

"Road Hockey" by Bruce Meyer is published with the permission of the author and Black Moss Press publishers of *Radio Silence*, 1991.

Michael Ondaatje's "To A Sad Daughter" appeared in *The Cinnamon Peeler* published by McClelland and Stewart in 1987. It appears here thanks to permission by the author and Ellen Levine Literary Agency/Trident Media Group.

Al Purdy's "Hockey Players" appears courtesy of Harbour Publishing.

Lyrics for "The Ballad of Wendel Clark" by the Rheostatics Part I by Martin Tielli and Part II by Dave Clark and Dave Bedini appear courtesy of the authors.

"Ice Time" by Ken Rivard appears by permission of the author.

"In Shape," "Goin Down," "Once is Once Too Many," "New Season," and "Johnny" by Stephen Scriver are published here courtesy of the author.

The words and music to "Hockey" are by Jane Siberry (1987) and the lyrics appear here thanks to Jane Siberry and Wing-it Music.

Birk Sproxton's "The Hockey Fan Reflects on Beginnings," "A Stitch in Time," "The Song of the Stay-at-Home Defenceman," and "First Blood, 1950" appear here by permission of the author.

"Thin Ice" by Betsy Struthers was first published in *That Sign of Perfection: From Bandy Legs to Beer Legs* edited by John B. Lee, Black Moss Press, 1995 and later in *Virgin Territory* published by Wolsak and Wynn in Toronto in 1996. It appears here with permission of the author.

"Fifty Mission Cap" by The Tragically Hip © 1992 by Little Smoke Music/ Peermusic Canada Inc. International copyright secured. All rights reserved. Used by permission.

Contents

Acknowledgements   5
Foreword   9
Preface   10
Introduction   11

More Than a Game   17
   I Am Hockey. MICHAEL P.J. KENNEDY   19
   The Hockey Song. STOMPIN' TOM CONNORS   23
   In Shape. STEPHEN SCRIVER   24
   Hockey Players. AL PURDY   25
   Coach's Corner. RICHARD HARRISON   27
   Road Hockey. BRUCE MEYER   28
   In The Hockey Hall of Fame I Sat Down and Wept. ROGER BELL   29
   My Father quit Hockey one Night Late in his Youth. JOHN B. LEE   31
   What It Takes. RICHARD HARRISON   32
   Me Like Hockey. THE ARROGANT WORMS   33
   Breakaway Sonnet. NILS CLAUSSON   34

Life Reflected in Ice   35
   The Skater. SIR CHARLES G.D. ROBERTS   37
   Hockey. JANE SIBERRY   38
   New Season. STEPHEN SCRIVER   39
   New Skates. C.H. (MARTY) GERVAIS   41
   The Hockey Fan Reflects On Beginnings. BIRK SPROXTON 43
   Christmas Hockey Game, Faculty versus Students
     (for Al Purdy). JOHN B. LEE   44
   Thin Ice. BETSY STRUTHERS   45
   Hockey Skates. KATHLEEN EDWARDS   46
   Defence Mechanisms. RICHARD HARRISON   47
   Thaw. MARGARET AVISON   48
   To A Sad Daughter. MICHAEL ONDAATJE   49
   A Stitch in Time. BIRK SPROXTON   51

Home Ice Advantage 53
First Blood, 1950. BIRK SPROXTON 55
Behind the Red Brick House (Charlottetown, P.E.I. 1955).
  HUGH MACDONALD 56
Family Pond. FLORENCE MCNEIL 58
When I Was a Boy and the Family Pond Froze. JOHN B. LEE 59
Ice Time. KEN RIVARD 60
At the arena. KELLEY JO BURKE 61
Classic City Arena on Friday Nights. BARRY BUTSON 62
Arena. DON GUTTERIDGE 63
Rink. JOAN FINNIGAN 64

Winners and Losers 66
The Hockey Player Sonnets (for Al Purdy). JOHN B. LEE 68
Dragging Buses With Your Teeth. C.H. (MARTY) GERVAIS 69
Anecdote of the Hockey Game. GERALD HILL 71
Summer Hockey Camp. DONNA KANE 72
The B-P-T. GARY HYLAND 73
The Song of the Stay-at-Home Defenceman. BIRK SPROXTON 75
Once Is Once Too Many. STEPHEN SCRIVER 77
Goin Down. STEPHEN SCRIVER 78
Canadian Angels. LORNA CROZIER 79
Rhéaume. RICHARD HARRISON 80
The Ballad of Wendel Clark. (THE RHEOSTATICS)
  Part I. MARTIN TIELLI
  Part II. DAVE CLARK AND DAVE BIDINI 81
To an Athlete Dying Young. A.E. HOUSMAN 83
Fifty Mission Cap. THE TRAGICALLY HIP 84
Dying on the Ice at 39 is Hard. JOHN B. LEE 85
Fogarty. RICHARD HARRISON 86
Johnny. STEPHEN SCRIVER 87
Grey is the Forelock Now of the Irishman. JOAN FINNIGAN 88

Roster of Authors 91
Hockey Literature Bibliography 101

Foreword

Hockey holds a special place in my heart. It has fascinated me for many years. Although at times it can be a rugged, brutal game, it is a swift, elegant, graceful game as well.

How can we ever forget the images of Yvan Cournoyer streaking through centre ice at top speed or Bobby Clarke and that gap-toothed grin staring down his opponent in the face-off circle? These are images indelibly etched in our minds.

Literature has held this same kind of grip over me ever since I can remember. Even today, I seemingly never go anywhere without something in my hand to read.

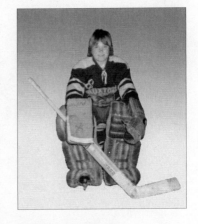

Kelly Hrudey as a pee wee.
Courtesy of Kelly Hrudey

Bringing the two together is the perfect powerplay. Like a well-executed man advantage, these two combined, click just right.

I love stories about people. Don't give me boring statistics; give me real stories about feelings and passion like "Road Hockey" by Bruce Meyer. I relived my very own childhood road hockey games played on the chilly streets of Edmonton reading his poem. Virtually each piece had me stop and recollect childhood memories before continuing on; tales about new skates, old arenas, stale popcorn, and nattily dressed fans.

Michael P. J. Kennedy has once again put together an all-star team that literary and hockey fans alike will cherish for generations.

Kelly Hrudey
Calgary, Alberta

Preface

When I was playing hockey, real men and real boys did not wear masks...we did not fear the puck. In those days, real men, real boys did not cry. When, through my felt pad a slapshot almost broke my shinbone, if I may say so, I kept my tears under my cheeks!

That was a long time ago. Now, real men, real boys wear masks. Often during my trips all over Canada, I have been invited to visit shrines dedicated to hockey. Showing me, in their basement, the sacred objects they have collected, real men, who had been real boys, sometimes do not

Roch Carrier in the "dreaded" Leafs sweater.
Library and Archives Canada © Public Domain. Courtesy of Roch Carrier's family. nlc–1789

conceal a tear when they are reminiscing about their game. In our country, no matter how triumphant they might be, all men have, in their hearts, some little scar from hockey.

On the other hand, is it not wonderful to foresee that more and more real girls, real women, now getting involved in hockey, will be able to share and trade memories about the experience of growing up and taming winter, in the excitement of this great game?

A friend of mine, who was a great poet and a fan of the now defunct Quebec Nordiques, used to proclaim that the best Canadian literature was written on the ice, by the hockey players, in the sophisticated calligraphy of their skates.

In this anthology, poets are really assuming their duty towards our great game—they remember and they celebrate it. After reading this anthology, put it under your pillow; it will give you beautiful dreams!

Roch Carrier
Westmount, Quebec

Introduction

When I first proposed developing a class entitled "Reading Culture: Hockey in Canadian Literature" at University of Saskatchewan in fall 2001, a number of people questioned whether there was enough Canadian hockey poetry and prose to offer a university-level class. Having done months of research, my answer was a resounding "Yes!" Indeed, there were more than enough poems, stories, essays, and, to a lesser extent, novels and plays to include in the class. If there was a problem, it lay in assembling these works since they were scattered throughout a number of different anthologies, individual collections, and stand-alone publications. Part of this problem was alleviated when I completed editing *Words on Ice: A Collection of Hockey Prose* which appeared in 2003. Now, with the appearance of *Going Top Shelf: An Anthology of Canadian Hockey Poetry*, much of our country's best hockey poetry and song lyrics have been collected as well.

Played at its highest level, hockey is arguably the most demanding of team sports. Indeed, for an individual player to maintain control of a sliding puck through the dexterous manipulation of a stick while that player is skating on ice at full speed is in itself an accomplishment. To do so while trying to evade one, two, or more 200 lb defenders whose mission is to use their bodies and sticks to relieve the puck-carrier of the small rubber disk, is an even more admirable feat. Yet for a player to do the above and then successfully go for the "top shelf;" to shoot the puck accurately into the net within a space barely visible above the body and extended hand of the goaltender, is a laudable feat achieved by few players on a regular basis.

For writers to create works which are at once engaging for a variety of readers yet contain sufficient intellectual and emotional merit to withstand critical and popular scrutiny, is for them to create poetry of artistic excellence which reaches the literary "top shelf."

For Canadians, hockey has a cultural significance which extends beyond a mere sporting activity. The hockey poetry and musical lyrics contained in this collection are the product of over thirty different authors from across Canada and reflect an intriguing diversity of forms and literary expression. Yet in all the poems, ice, or the sport which is played so extensively in Canada upon it, is used to give voice to the ideas, beliefs, and attitudes of this diverse group of Canadian authors. In my judgement, this collection represents a literary "top shelf" of hockey poetry without equal.

The collection is divided into four sections, yet despite the commercialization of hockey the connection among the works contained within each section may appear, at times, somewhat tenuous. Indeed, the initial section, MORE THAN A GAME begins with a work that is not even a poem! "I Am Hockey" is an essay which will place this anthology into perspective within our collective Canadian self-concept.

Just as there are different levels of hockey ranging from Olympic and professional to Major Junior, university, and amateur, so too the world reflected in each poem and song contained in the section MORE THAN A GAME is diverse. In its most straightforward way, the game is captured in Tom Connors' "The Hockey Song," an anthem to the game played and sung countless times each day in arenas across the country, and in The Arrogant Worms' "Me Like Hockey." Stephen Scriver's "In Shape" gets to the heart of what it is to be caught up in the individual physical preparation for the game. Beyond this is the essence of what it is to be Canadian by playing the game as captured in Al Purdy's timeless "Hockey Players" and Richard Harrison's "What It Takes." For some, the sport becomes a metaphor for the passing of a part of life. This is reflected in "Road Hockey" by Bruce Meyer, "In The Hockey Hall of Fame I Sat Down And Wept" by Roger Bell, and "My Father Quit Hockey One Night Late In His Youth" by John B. Lee. The larger than life figure of Don Cherry is seen in "Coach's Corner" by Harrison and the section concludes with Nils Clausson's light tribute to the creative player in hockey, "Breakaway Sonnet."

LIFE REFLECTED IN ICE is more than a group of poems which hold up a mirror to reality. The ice described often distorts reality, but it does capture several interesting aspects of life ranging from the power of nature, to the mutability of existence, to the joy and optimism humans can exhibit, to abject disappointment. Romantic poet Charles G.D. Roberts captures the awesome experience of skating alone in Nature; of being alone in the presence of our great Northland in "The Skater." Jane Siberry's "Hockey" reminisces about holding onto games of old, real games of shinny perhaps, which once gone, like the youth of those who played, are gone forever. Similar reminiscence is to be found in Marty Gervais' "New Skates." Stephen Scriver's optimisim and celebration of human spirit are reflected in the exhuberance of "New Season." Birk Sproxton has fun with his memory of hockey in Flin Flon, Manitoba in "The Hockey Fan Reflects on Beginnings," while John B. Lee describes with warm feelings ongoing days of hockey in "Christmas Hockey Game, Faculty versus Students."

"Thin Ice" by Betsy Struthers, "Hockey Skates" by Kathleen Edwards, "Defence Mechanisms" by Richard Harrison, and "Thaw" by Margaret Avison all illustrate the less attractive side of life as ice and skates and hockey are used to describe relationships. Yet the section ends with the powerful poem of acceptance and love entitled "To A Sad Daughter" by Michael Ondaatje, and Sproxton's whimsical yet philosophical poem of acceptance and personal growth called "A Stich in Time" where adversity develops the individual.

HOME ICE ADVANTAGE examines all the places where the game is played, from the first rink on the street in ball hockey described in "First Blood, 1950" by Birk Sproxton, to the drained park pool for shinny in Ken Rivard's "Ice Time." Whether it is the backyard rink of "Behind the Red Brick House" by Hugh MacDonald or the ponds of "Family Pond" by Florence McNeil or "When I Was a Boy and the Farm Pond Froze" by John B. Lee, each locale has something that makes it unique and memorable. Kelley Jo Burke's small town arena and its denizens are captured well in "At The Arena," as are the sights and sounds of the urban rink in "Classic City Arena on Friday Night" by Barry Butson. For some, the buildings in which the game has been played take on special meaning as they celebrate the incomparable Rocket Richard in

"Arena" by Don Gutteridge and Ottawa Senator star Frank Finnigan in "Rink" by his daughter, Joan Finnigan.

The collection concludes with WINNERS AND LOSERS which examines the psychology of sports' victories and loses and those who experience them—players and fans alike. The frustration of supporting a continually losing team and the travails of playing amateur hockey under less than ideal conditions are joined in John B. Lee's "The Hockey Player Sonnets." "The only thing I was good at was table hockey," starts Marty Gervais' "Dragging Buses With Your Teeth," but the poem does show how there may be hope for the next generation to succeed! "Anecdote of the Hockey Game" by Gerald Hill and Donna Kane's "Summer Hockey Camp" reinforce the optimism parents or members of the older generation have for youthful players who are the future of the game and the future of society. Gary Hyland's "The B-P-T" illustrates how even players with limited skills and low self-concept can at times be "winners," while the blueliner in Birk Sproxton's "The Song of the Stay-at-Home Defenceman," the screening forward in "Once Is Once Too Many," and the hapless shot-blocker in "Goin Down" (both by Stephen Scriver) illustrate well the pitfalls of the sport. Lorna Crozier sings the praises of Canada's Women's Olympic Hockey team of 2002 in "Canadian Angels," and Richard Harrison in "Rheaume" and The Rheostatics in "The Ballad of Wendel Clark" praise two of the game's notable performers. In the only work by a non-Canadian in the collection, Victorian English poet A.E. Housman reminds readers of the brevity of fame in "To An Athlete Dying Young." One such athlete was the Toronto Maple Leafs' 1951 Stanley Cup game-winning scorer, Bill Barilko, who never played another game, was killed in an airplane crash. His story is captured in The Tragically Hip's "Fifty Mission Cap." Less dramatic, yet nonetheless just as tragic, is the loss of life at an early age presented in John B. Lee's "Dying on the Ice at 39 is Hard." "Fogarty" by Richard Harrison laments the loss of so much potential with the real-life story of one of junior hockey's most talented graduates, Brian Fogarty. Stephen Scriver also captures the theme of lost potential and all that might have been, in what might be called "To An Athlete Dying Old" in his poem "Johnny." The collection concludes with

Joan Finnigan writing about her father in "Grey Is The Forelock Now Of The Irishman" and how he has survived as a mere shadow of what he once was when he was a pre-eminent National Hockey League star. Yet in her eyes, the eyes of a daughter, he remains a star.

Yes, there are numerous poems about hockey—diverse, entertaining, and intellectually stimulating poems. Read them and enjoy them as over thirty different authors have contributed over three dozen individual works to create a truly "Top Shelf" collection of Canadian hockey poetry.

Michael P.J. Kennedy, Ph.D.
Vanscoy, Saskatchewan, 2005

MORE THAN A GAME

Boys playing hockey in Edmonton. (Glenbow Archives NC–6–12373b)

"I Am Hockey"
Michael P.J. Kennedy

I am a logical man. In fact, when I am teaching my university classes, I always say to my students: "Take a stance!" "Express your own opinion, but always provide logical support."

It must be thirty-five years since I was a first-year university student who sat in philosophy class entranced by a small figure of a man with a dark beard, horn-rimmed glasses, and a blue suit. "What *is* reality?" he would ask. "How do you know that you exist?" For three hours each week in Philosophy 101, I had my "real world" challenged. This experience helped me to develop as a thinking person and to appreciate a world based on logical thought. Then there were those syllogisms ...

According to the *Oxford Canadian Dictionary*, a syllogism is "a form of reasoning in which a conclusion is drawn from two given or assumed propositions (premises): a common or middle term is present in the two premises but not in the conclusion" (Toronto: Oxford University Press, 1998: 1469). In short, if A = B and C = B, then logically, rationally, intellectually A = C! However, as my esteemed professor was quick to demonstrate, some of these logical conclusions were questionable at best. Indeed, I learned that logic is not always as simple as it might appear to be. For example, if some men have beards, and seals have beards, does it mean that some men are seals?

All of this came back to me in the fall of 2003 when I was being interviewed by a journalist who was interested in my new collection of hockey prose. "Why do you like hockey so much? What does the sport mean to you?" he asked.

I immediately responded by saying something like: "Hockey is Canada" or "Hockey is Canadian." But the more I thought about it, the more I realized that my response regarding Canada's official winter sport was more than something to be inscribed on tee shirts or to be blurted out in Pavlovian dog-like fashion. Hockey for most Canadians does mean something beyond its role as sport or entertainment. After all, our non-winter official sport, lacrosse, doesn't stir up the same sensibility as hockey. Yet how extensive is hockey's grip on Canadians?

For me, hockey had always been an interesting sport, but one for which I have demonstrated very little talent. Sure, I can skate—forward at least, and at an early age I understood that Toronto was the only team worth rooting for even if Montreal won all the Stanley Cups. It wasn't until I was in graduate school that I truly came to understand the impact of hockey on our citizenry.

In 1971–72 I was studying for my doctorate in Canadian Literature at University of Ottawa. I had recently completed my first year of classes while concurrently teaching my initial university-level course. A late summer camping trip to the Maritimes took me through New Brunswick, onto Prince Edward Island, and into Nova Scotia including Cape Breton Island. It was while on this foray into Canada's East that I began to understand the depth of hockey's influence on our people.

Nineteen seventy-two was a year that most Canadians alive at the time will never forget. It was a year not unlike 1967, the year of Canada's centennial and Expo 67, which defined for many of us who we were within the global community. The "Summit Series," Canada versus the Soviet Union in hockey, featured the remarkable comeback which will forever define Canadian grit and determination. But before the euphoria of victory, there was the pall of defeat across the land. Indeed, as I ventured into the East, all that people discussed was the series. At a campground in Cape Breton or a service station in PEI the feelings were the same. We were all Canadians whether from Ontario or Nova Scotia, farmer, fisher, or student, we shared in our collective shock, sadness, and perhaps anger at the early success of the Soviet team. "I knew we were not very good at much," said a disappointed young patron in a Charlottetown pub. "But I always thought we were the best in hockey." Throughout the trip, people came together to share the disappointments and the small victories of our team as we faced the Russians.

By the time the series had relocated to Europe for the final four games in the Soviet Union, I was back in Ottawa. September classes had begun and I was assigned a class entitled "Canadian Literature for French-Speaking Students." The new semester meant new responsibilities for me in only my second year of university teaching. As a teaching fellow I was taking Ph.D. classes while providing instruction to a full class of over thirty-five students. Yet the "Summit Series" was never far away from daily thoughts and conversations for us all. With game eight, the series came down to one game, the last chance for Canada to pull out a series victory.

Where was I when Paul Henderson scored that magnificent goal to capture the series? I was *supposed to be* in a classroom teaching my class. However I made a decision that I will never regret. I looked at my fellow Canadians as we assembled for the class and said: "We don't want to be here, do we? Let's go down to the student lounge and watch the game!" And what a game it was. At the end, we cheered, and many of us had tears in our eyes. Outside in the streets surrounding Ottawa U. it was as if we had been victorious in war. Horns honked, and people cheered and we all knew this game of hockey extended far, far beyond the logic of a physical sport enjoyed as entertainment. It was an intrinsic part of us all, as throughout Canada, Francophone and Anglophone, student and teacher, Maritimer and Central Canadian shared in the victory.

In subsequent years I have enjoyed the sport as a spectator and as a sports journalist. I have witnessed countless university and college games, professional games in every NHL city including Quebec and Winnipeg, and very special games such as NHL playoffs and Canada Cup games. Each game has reinforced my belief that the sport has an effect on us which extends beyond the event itself. Yet despite the periodic elation generated within the country at World Junior Championships and Canada or World Cup tournaments, does the country truly define itself by the sport?

Logically I know from doing research for an article I wrote in 1998 entitled "Hockey as Metaphor in Canadian Literature" that hockey has influenced our literature. There is also evidence of the impact of the sport on our music and visual art. Nevertheless, as the new century has begun in an increasingly multicultural Canada, perhaps the "good old days" of hockey are gone forever. After all, Canadian participants in other sports seem to be placing themselves on the world stage in competition, whether it is professional basketball, baseball, and golf or amateur women's soccer.

In 2001 I did extensive research and developed curriculum for a class to be taught at University of Saskatchewan as part of the English Department's "Reading Culture" series. "Reading Culture: Animals," "Reading Culture: Railways," and "Reading Culture: Education" had all been proposed. What I developed and what was accepted was: "Reading Culture: Hockey in Canadian Literature." I was not sure what to expect. I knew there were enough quality texts to read and study, but would I be able to recruit enough students to take the class?

Since its first appearance in September 2002, the class has proven immensely popular and each semester since it was first offered, the class has been full. Regularly during the first week or two of each semester there are six, seven, or more students meeting me in hallways, e-mailing me, or phoning me trying to get into the class. Even when it was offered during the usually slower spring session, it filled up to capacity. At the conclusion of each class I teach, I have students complete an anonymous course evaluation. In over thirty years of post-secondary teaching I have rarely seen a class which has been so universally well received by students. Although I would like to take credit for being an immensely popular instructor, I know from specific questions on the student evaluations that more and more of the students are taking the class because it is "the hockey class." Who are these students? Those who enrol are from a variety of colleges within the university. Women and men (in approximately equal numbers) have come from the College of Commerce, College of Arts and Science, Nursing, Engineering, and Agriculture with only a few from Kinesiology. In other words, it is not just the "jocks" looking for an easy class. In reality, the class is one of the most demanding English classes in terms of reading and writing assignments.

Students learn what any students should learn in a literature and composition class: how to read, analyze, and discuss logically works of poetry, fiction, and drama. Yet each of the works discussed deals with hockey. Participants also learn how to develop written arguments in formal English and how to document their arguments within a well-written essay. However the course does provide students with additional work from non-fiction, especially autobiography, biography, and sports journalism. Whatever the genre studied, hockey is the vehicle upon which classroom discussions are based. By the conclusion of the class, students can see how pervasive the sport is within the Canadian cultural fabric.

Hockey remains a big part of most contemporary students' cognitive framework. If the dozens of students who have appeared in my classes to date are any evidence, the sport remains a real part of who they are. While some students may enjoy playing the sport at present and others are avid spectators, virtually all of the Canadian students in each of these classes know the joy of skating on an outdoor rink or on a slough. They may have the world of international sports and entertainment at their fingertips through satellite television, computer graphics, and the Internet, yet for most of these young people, hockey is synonymous with being Canadian. These young adults may not have been alive in 1972, yet when the subject of 2002 Olympics comes up in class, they are eager to relate where they were and what they were doing as Canada's men's and women's hockey teams captured the 2002 Olympic Gold medals. For the current generation of young people, 2002 is their 1972.

Beyond the students enrolled in this class, there are countless Canadians from all walks of life who share strong feelings for the sport. A prime example is the impact felt by the "Heritage Classic" games in Edmonton in October 2003 where 57,167 individuals sat in freezing temperatures to watch two old-fashioned games of outdoor hockey while over 2.7 million other Canadians watched on television. Hall of Fame players donned toques and shovelled snow from the ice surface between periods in what was billed a "Mega-Stars" game of retired Edmonton Oilers vs. former Montreal Canadiens. Following this contest, a regular NHL game was played between the current Oilers and Canadiens on the outdoor rink in the middle of Commonwealth Stadium.

For the players, the old timers especially, it might have been considered an opportunity to see old friends. But for many it went beyond that to the heart of what the game itself means to us as Canadians. The night before the "Mega-Stars" contest Wayne Gretzky said: Hockey is "the greatest game in the world and we never grow tired of it." Erstwhile Montreal forward and member of the Hall of Fame Steve Shutt explained the popularity of the upcoming outdoor game as "people going back to their roots. Everybody grew up on an outdoor rink and I think this stripped down hockey takes the business away from it, all the marketing, as you just go back to like when everyone was a kid playing pond hockey. I think that's what's caught everybody's imagination."

Former Canadiens defenceman Guy Lapointe saw the event as "for the people ... [it] brings back memories of when we were kids." Dave Hunter, an Oilers alumnus known more for his hard-nosed play than high skill, also saw the contest as "for the fans" and found it exciting, indeed, "just great to be with the fellows again."

More than a friendly alumni game for two teams of aging retirees, the outdoor nature of the game attracted people from across the country in an illogical yet understandable way. Two unemployed young men from Labrador, for example, were recently laid off from their jobs, not knowing where they would find money for groceries in a week. Yet they were there. "It was a no-brainer" according to them, to make the trek from Eastern Canada by bus. There was an entire family; mother, father, son, and daughter from Winnipeg who wanted to experience this outdoor event. There was a "just married" couple from Windsor, Ontario on their honeymoon. When the man was asked why they were there, he pointed to his smiling bride and said "It was her idea!" The disparate nature of who was there extended to four retired buddies who have known each other for decades who flew from central Ontario to be at this unique sporting event. Why come sit in the cold (-19 and colder) stadium to see from a considerable distance former NHL stars play a game that had no meaning beyond nostalgia and then sit for hours more watching two mediocre NHL teams play on the same outdoor rink? Why did the senior and his middle-aged son travel for hours from Grande Prairie in the north to huddle together in sleeping bags or the two young men come north from Moose Jaw layered in ski-doo suits and blankets just to sit in unshovelled snow at their feet on cold, cold seats? Come to think of it, what logical reason did I have for spending time and money travelling from Saskatoon to Calgary to Edmonton for the better part of a day in a cramped airplane for the pleasure of sitting for six additional hours in the cold?

Logic? The logic is there, of course, as any real Canadian would know. Hockey is Canada. I am Canadian. Therefore it is crystal clear ... I am Hockey!

The Hockey Song
Stompin' Tom Connors

Hello out there we're on the air it's hockey night tonight
Tension grows the whistle blows and the puck goes down the ice.
The goalie jumps and the players bump and the fans all go insane
Someone roars "Bobby scores!" at the good ole hockey game.

Chorus:
Oh the good ole hockey game is the best game you can name
And the best game you can name is the good ole hockey game

2nd period:
Where players dash with skates aflash the home team trails behind
But they grab the puck and go bursting up and they're down across the line.
They storm the crease like bumble bees they travel like a burning flame
We see them slide the puck inside—It's a "1–1" hockey game!

Chorus:
Oh the good ole hockey game is the best game you can name
And the best game you can name is the good ole hockey game

3rd period: last game in the playoffs, too ...
Oh take me where the hockey players face off down the rink—
And the Stanley Cup is all filled up for the chaps who win the drink—
Now the final flick of the hockey stick and a gigantic scream—
The puck is in! The home team wins! The good ole hockey game!

Chorus:
Oh the good ole hockey game is the best game you can name
And the best game you can name is the good ole hockey game

He shoots he scores.

In Shape
Stephen Scriver

just to move, man
feel those muscles stir again
long summer of beer and sun

just to move
hear the old heart pounding
full of one more season

feel the body burst again
charged with easy sweat

two weeks of up, down
            up, down
                backwards, forwards
blow that whistle, man
sounds like music now it's easy

... move, man
only six strides down now
blue/white/red/white/blue/white
around the net
leg over leg
and blue/white/red ...

lungs smooth with swelling breath
legs pump   push that ice again

ah, but just to move

Hockey Players
Al Purdy

What they worry about most is injuries
          broken arms and legs and
fractured skulls opening so doctors
can see such bloody beautiful things almost
not quite happening in the bone rooms
          as they happen outside
And the referee?
          He's right there on the ice
not out of sight among the roaring blue gods
of a game played for passionate stockbrokers
children wearing business suits
and a nation of television agnostics
who never agree with the referee and applaud
when he falls flat on his face

          On a breakaway
the centreman carrying the puck
his wings trailing a little
          on both sides why
I've seen the aching glory of a resurrection
          in their eyes
          if they score
but crucifixions agony to lose
—the game?

          We sit up there in the blues
bored and sleepy and suddenly three men
break down the ice in roaring feverish speed and
we stand up in our seats with such a rapid pouring
of delight exploding out of self to join them why
theirs and our orgasm is the rocket stipend
for skating thru the smoky end boards out
of sight and climbing up the appalachian highlands
and racing breast to breast across laurentian barrens
over hudson's diamond bay and down the treeless tundra where
auroras are tubercular and awesome and
stopping isn't feasible or possible or lawful
but we have to and we have to
          laugh because we must and
stop to look at self and one another but
          our opponent's never geography
               or distant why
        it's men
        —just men?

And how do the players feel about it
this combination of ballet and murder?
For years a Canadian specific
to salve the anguish of inferiority
by being good at something the Americans aren't
And what's the essence of a game like this
which takes a ten year fragment of a man's life
replaced with love that lodges in his brain
            and substitutes for reason?
Besides the fear of injuries
is it the difficulty of ever really overtaking
a hard black rubber disc?
—Boys playing a boy's game in a permanent childhood
with screaming coach who insists on winning
sports-writer-critics and the crowd gone mad?
—And the worrying wives wanting you to quit and
your aching body stretched on the rubbing table
thinking of money in owners' pockets that might be yours
the butt-slapping camaraderie and the self indulgence
of allowing yourself to be a hero and knowing
everything ends in a pot-belly

Out on the ice can all these things be forgotten
in swift and skilled delight of speed?
—roaring out the end boards out the city
streets and high up where laconic winds
whisper litanies for a fevered hockey player
Or racing breast to breast and never stopping
over rooftops of the world and all together
sing the song of winning all together
sing the song of money all together

            (and out in the suburbs
there's the six-year-old kid
whose reflexes were all wrong
who always fell down and hurt himself and cried
and never learned to skate
            with his friends)

Coach's Corner

Richard Harrison

The almost clerical collar, he is the priest of rock 'em
sock 'em. He silences his more knowledgeable friends
with his faith in the bodies of men and without him
and his kind the NHL would be vapid as the All-Star
Game forever. He is loud and whiny and complaining
and chokes up on air if he's hurt by someone's words—
everything a man should not be, yet every sports bar
wills itself to quiet, turns up the volume on its dozen
sets only for his words. He is their man in a way no
hero of the play could be; his big league career was a
single game, but remember, he used to tell Bobby Orr
what to do and Bobby listened as we listen though we
let the game go on in silence. He slams foreigners,
praises women in all the ways wrong for our time,
rejects any wavering in the masculinity of his troops
like a colonel in the US Marines. And yet he is here
because he is unafraid to love, love the game, the
journeyman players, love the code that makes a man a
man and if you don't know, I ain't gonna tell ya. He
loves the fans, for all the pain they cause him, and we
are here with our own uncomfortable backs for that
dogged love, the voice that rises like a tenor sax,
pointed fingers, eyes narrowed to see clear and deep
the world that has him trapped on two sides already.

Road Hockey
Bruce Meyer

The middle of my journey,
as the train shakes,
I wake from a dream
about my childhood
where I saw the boys
I played hockey with
on the frozen streets
beneath purple dusks.
Snow had settled
on the brown furrows
of the fall ploughings
the way a dusting of ice
clung to our corduroys
as we shouted and raved
in a dead-end street,
pushing and hacking
each other's spindly legs
until the night descended
blackening the game
and calling us home
to those tiny rooms
taped with clippings
of Howe and Hull
and silver grails.
I wanted to go back there,
wanted to dream again
of what I would become
but only became
the things I am
regardless of the dreams.
And as I woke just now,
at some point in a journey
I realized we'd all
become grown men,
and the waking, not the growing
left me angry. Snow whirls
by the coach car window,
still clings to the furrows
of pantlegs and fields
as the journeymen continue on
their battles of earthly overtime
and the sudden darkness
after.

In The Hockey Hall of Fame I Sat Down and Wept
Roger Bell

Foolish in a man of my age, perhaps,
but Beehive Corn Syrup
Tim Horton brushcut and
Jacques Plante diving and
cards and coins and pennants
and echoes in my chest turned on some ache
so I sat down on the bench of sighs

and wept for narrow beds shared with brothers
pillowed borders down the middle and
elbows in the night if you strayed over

and I wept for simple Saturdays
in theatres with matinees and
pink elephant popcorn
cliffhangers and shouting

and I wept for Roy Rogers twin six-shooters
low on my hips and how fast I was

and for drawers and drawers of comic books read
and reread under the rain-pelted roof

and I wept for balloon tires
riding through the leaves of fall
long after dark when bonfires filled the air
and mothers called

and green apple fights

and my first cat dying
and Norma Lynn Gallagher on the back of my tricycle
with the handlebar streamers painting the day

and I wept for Roy's Confectionary
three candies for a cent and the half-dollar sack
Robert McKay and I bought, heavy as pirate gold
and ate in the dark of Friday films
under the prowling nose of Mrs. Lesperance

and Ella Bolander's coffee cake
still warm and sugar brown
and Mackenzies' milkshakes
served cold and threescoop thick
by summer girls with hair in braids

and I wept for the night
I touched Rocket Richard
and found out he was only flesh

and I wept and wept for the way breath seems
on the sharp froze river of December dawn
to just slip away, transparent, like all those years
so easily

and is gone

My Father Quit Hockey One Night Late in his Youth

John B. Lee

My father quit hockey
one night late in his youth.
Went home
and hung his skates in the shed
told his young bride
he was done with the game.

Done with the time he would race
a catalogue bent round each shin
and the wind in his face.
Done with the crack of the puck
and the rush-cut of the blade.
Done with the music of heart in the head.
Done with the sanguine age
when winter had a joy to rival the summer's sun.

He still tells the story
of one luckless player
who lived out his days a broken doll
heart quietly ticking
like a great clock lost in a corner.

But as for me
I feel a sadness that cannot grieve
and like a wicked son
I risk unmendable memory
and play the game beyond
the reach of wisdom in my ever collapsing years.

What It Takes

—for Bernie Federko, on the occasion of his induction into the
    Hockey Hall of Fame, November, 2002.
Richard Harrison

Any Saskatchewan kid who lays his head
on the dark earth dreaming in a crown of brome
can find it in the sweater he brought to Foam Lake
trimmed the colours of the prairie sky in summer.
And the men who picked enough roots and stones
from their father's land to tell could see it when
they rested by the boards and watched him
practice on the rink—Don't forget the work.
Take the ice the way you enter a room. Learn
everyone by name. When you have the puck,
more often than not, the goal is another man away.
Give everything its place. When he was named
to the Hall of Fame, first thing Bernie did
was call his friends, and in a voice still shocked
with unexpected joy, give away what
a thousand games of pro will teach a man who listens:
You do your best, he said, *but you never know.*

Me Like Hockey
The Arrogant Worms

Me work hard 5 days a week
Sweeping garbage from the street
Come home not want book to read
Not 'nuff pictures for me see
Sit right down in favourite chair
Wearing only underwear
Favourite night is Saturday night
'Cause me can watch hockey fights

Me Like Hockey!

Me not like pro basketball
'Cause me short and they all tall
Baseball slow like Forrest Gump
'Cept when Robby spits on ump
Wrestlemania not so great
Me like to see Hulk Hogan skate
TV soccer not so hot
You play bad then you get shot

Me Like Hockey!

Swedish players must be geeks
'Cause they still got own real teeth
Not like Finnish players names
What's a Teemu anyways?
Russians worse in history
Got stupid names like Valery
Me like Sergei Federov
Me like him more if head were off
ha! ha! ha!

Me Like Hockey!

Please Mr. Linesman let the players fight

Friends come over put game on
Argue then we lay bets down
Got bag of chips and case of Bud
Should last till end of first period
But Yankees they win the World Cup
Me think they cheat use glowy puck!
Maybe if we want to win her
Maybe we should play in winter

Me Like Hockey!

Breakaway Sonnet
Nils Clausson

… at 19:20 the harassed centre
loses, ineptly, the rebellious puck
to the alert just turning defenceman
stickhandles beside around the caught off-

guard left-wing and fluid as a dancer's
leap eludes crosses spots his breaking right-
wing draws it in as if on a taut string
streaks to the last defender then backhands

to his own alone (as if in a field
of summer wheat) defenceman bursts goalward
feints with head and hips making the goalie
commit himself too soon he shoots he scores

and turns arms high to the cheering hearts stirred
in the place where the poem has occurred.

LIFE REFLECTED IN ICE

Eva Ault, January 1917. (Library and Archives Canada/William James Topley collection/PA–043029 © Public Domain. nlc-5767)

The Skater

Sir Charles G.D. Roberts

My glad feet shod with the glittering steel
I was the god of the winged heel.[1]

The hills in the far white sky were lost;
The world lay still in the wide white frost;

And the woods hung hushed in their long white dream
By the ghostly, glimmering, ice-blue stream.

Here was a pathway, smooth like glass,
Where I and the wandering wind might pass

To the far-off palaces, drifted deep,
Where Winter's retinue rests in sleep.

I followed the lure, I fled like a bird,
Till the startled hollows awoke and heard

A spinning whisper, a sibilant twang,
As the stroke of the steel on the tense ice rang;

And the wandering wind was left behind
As faster, faster I followed my mind;

Till the blood sang high in my eager brain,
And the joy of my flight was almost in pain.

Then I stayed the rush of my eager speed
And silently went as a drifting seed,—

Slowly, furtively, till my eyes
Grew big with the awe of a dim surmise,

And the hair of my neck began to creep
At hearing the wilderness talk in sleep.

Shapes in the fir-gloom drifted near.
In the deep of my heart I heard my fear.

And I turned and fled, like a soul pursued,
From the white, inviolate solitude.

---

1   in Greek mythology, Hermes, who was messenger of the gods

Hockey
Jane Siberry

winter time and the frozen river
sunday afternoon
they're playing hockey on the river
rosy …
he'll have that scar on his chin forever someday his girlfriend will say
hey where …
he might look out the window … or not
you skate as fast as you can 'til you hit the snowbank
(that's how you stop)
and you get your sweater from the catalogue
you use your rubber boots for goal posts
ah … walkin' home

don't let those sunday afternoons
get away get away get away get away
break away break away break away break away

this stick was signed by jean beliveau so don't fucking tell me where
     to fucking go …
oh sunday afternoon
someone's dog just took the puck—he buried it it's in the snowbank
     … your turn
they rioted in the streets of montreal when they benched rocket
     richard it's true

don't let those sunday afternoons
get away get away get away get away
break away break away break away break away

the sun is fading on the frozen river
the wind is dying down
someone else just got called for dinner
rosy
hmm … sunday afternoon

New Season
Stephen Scriver

Yer damn right it sill hurts
dislocated shoulder doesn't heal easy
damn near can't get a beer to my mouth

it's bin a long summer
thinking about those playoffs
an how the Monarchs did it to us again

but I got a feelin
we won't be second this time around
well, look—Archie's comin back
he wants another crack at Latourneau too
after the bugger speared him in that last game
an with both of us out
the team just rolled over and died

hell, so what if he's 38
he's only gotta skate half as far
to get as much done as most guys

an he's got this old buddy of his
coming outa Regina—name's Jeffreys—
played junior outa Estevan a few years ago
made it all the way to Rangers camp
before the bad pins caught up with him
but he'll look slick in this league

I know, Jimmy an Rick finally hung em up
but Jimmy took that one in the head
an Rick says he's too old to hack it anymore
an they both figger
we're never gonna beat the Monarchs
so the blue line looks mighty bare

but Mick's gonna be back
an he's too fat to play forward now anyways
an you know that kid Primrose—
played with the junior B's up in Ituna—
he says he'll be over
if Melville cuts him this fall

ya, Spike's gone from the pipes
but we bin talkin to this guy
from Summerberry—you know, Chambers—
sure he's old but he hasn't lost that much

ana couple more juveniles are movin up
they'll make it if they keep their heads up
an there's the rest of us—
another year older ana bit slower I guess
but so's everybody else—the Monarchs
included

ya, first practice next Friday—
you know, I got a feelin
if my shoulder holds out
this is gonna be our year

New Skates
C.H. (Marty) Gervais

When I see my young son pulling
on a pair of stiff new skates, I remember
a time just after Dief got elected
and we had moved to the north
and all my new friends were getting ready
for hockey season, and I had never played hockey
except on a road with running shoes
and a net make of potato sacks
At first, there was pride in watching my father
sharpen skates in the basement—sparks flying
about like fireflies—With great satisfaction,
he handed us those soft leather black ankle skates
that he had salvaged from an old cardboard box
found under the basement stairs
before we had left Windsor
and polished them army boot clean
and told us that by sharpening them himself
he had saved 25 cents at the arena
Said he could do just as good a job himself
But the edges were rough and uneven
and predictably, we fell flat on our asses
on the ice as our friends circled about us—
their laughter falling around us
as we silently cursed our father
who was down at the plant working
oblivious to our humiliation
We didn't tell him anything
because he would have yanked the skates
away from us and worked on them
until they felt sharp against his thumb
and we knew that wouldn't do any good
and he would have told us to get the polish
out and give them a good shine
but nobody ever polished skates
It was my mother who finally
carried the skates over to the skate shop
and learned from the owner
that nobody wore skates like that anymore—
in fact he hadn't seen any skates like that
since before the Second World War—
no ankle support and the leather so worn
that it was smooth as a glove,
and told her that somebody could get hurt with these
especially playing hockey

Reluctantly she bought us each a new pair
I remember running my hand over
the smooth leather and the hard toe
of the skates—they seemed
so perfectly formed, so fast
And all we needed now to save face
was to keep skating, to keep my father away
from the blades, to keep skating, never
to look behind, to keep right on moving

The Hockey Fan Reflects On Beginnings
Birk Sproxton

It all begins with guts. The looping scrawl of prairie rivers tucked inside the cavity of your belly, chewing your food, as they say munch, munch. Just chomping and chewing and squirting and squeezing and sqooshing mush diddle diddle mush, moving a lung, tickling the blood stream blood red, trickling along the vine of veins. Squish dee doodle go the guts. Squoik. Down the hatch, down the tube, the same old story: the teacher smears the ping pong ball with glycerine and squeezes it into the inner tube, bicycle tube, red with some blue blotches tries to squeeze it down the tube, muscles working, grimace, grunt, stuck in the old tube, slammed shut, bunged up. Guts belong in your belly and you want to leave them there where they belong. Don't spill them however much you long to tell it all.

In Flin Flon he begins another beginning, a legendary place where the garden is called, yes, the Main Arena and the streets are paved with hockey pucks and gold. Or so the story goes and you never get away from the stories. Right now, on the desk in front of me, a May 1989 article in *The Hockey News* tells how the Swift Current Broncos come from the smallest town to win the Memorial Cup since the Flin Flon Bombers won in 1957. You see? You *see?*

Flin Flon? they say.

Why the only people I know are from Flin Flon are hockey players and hookers.

My mother is from Flin Flon, you say.

Long pause.

And what position does she play?

Left Wing, Right Wing, Defence, Goal: the goal of life is.

Of course you expect stories from people raised in a town named after the nickname of a fictional hero. The hockey fan began in place and a good beginning it was. His mother worked hard to bear him. She carried him warm in her belly and then he was bare and she lugged him home in her arms. Her travail gave him from her to you, sitting there, lying there. A good beginning it was, but sometimes she can barely stand him.

Christmas Hockey Game, Faculty versus Students
—for Al Purdy
John B. Lee

Here on this ice
we skate,
each year
a little older
each year
a little greyer, a little slacker in the gut
and slower, as if age were a drug
with a long half-life
releasing minutes into the blood stream
till finally we will be sluggish
as smoked bees.

And each year the kids come at us
younger, fresher, stronger, more full of life,
always the same joke at the blue line,
always the same faces
off and rushing the net.

Some day we'll seize like rusty shears
or drawl like strings
winding down from unhooked kites
the puck will leap
and pass through insubstantial cavities
like a bird through light fog
where we look all cloudy
vapoured as we are upon exhausted frames
and whispering ghosts of former selves
but there too
the ghost of a happy boy.

Thin Ice
Betsy Struthers

All of us play at reconciliation,
a game of shinny on the backyard rink,
where bluelines shadow thin ice:

You and me and your daughter
against our husbands and my son.
Last year, it was family vs family

when you were still a family (Now
it's two on one, power plays, goals
missed and disputed)

Thwack of stick on stick, the shush of skates:
your husband crouched, ready to glove
any shot you try to get by him.

The kids have given up, cold feet, fed up
with the fights, you at one end, he
at the other, the two of us

circling between you, unwilling
to be audience or referees.
You've also had enough,

but he isn't ready to quit. The surface
chips under our blades, brings us
to our knees. Call it a draw

if you want. Or a victory. Whatever
it's time to be done with this, admit
that it's over

Hockey Skates

Kathleen Edwards

Going down in the same old town down the same street to the same bar
And the same old people saying hi and I don't care
Going down in the same old bar and I don't even order anymore
I am so sick of consequence and the look on your face
I am tired of playing defence
I don't even have hockey skates

You can meet me at ten thirty
I won't be there I'll be gone
We can talk like we are friends
Going over it all again
Talking about everything I am doing wrong

Do you wish your nose was longer
So you'd have an excuse not to see past it
Do you wish the lights were brighter in the city that you live
I am so sick of consequences.

Do you think your boys club will crumble
Just because of a loud-mouthed girl?

Defence Mechanisms
Richard Harrison

Because his jaw was broken when he knelt between
the shooter and the open net, he's vanished from the
line-up. Then the commentators say the team is better
off without him, and my anger rises: he gave everything
to that team he carried all year. Yet I catch myself
in the same words about the family I made and left.
We are talking these days about children, and the
bad example I set when I cut an apple, holding it
in my palm, and at last, cut my finger. I, who take
my hands from my pockets when I see a mother
carry her newborn across the threshold of the
subway door in case the baby falls, or the doors
begin to close. I, who once had four names to
offer with my own, and now say they are better
off without me.

Thaw
Margaret Avison

Sticky inside their winter suits
The Sunday children stare at pools
In pavement and black ice where roots
Of sky in moodier sky dissolve.

    An empty coach train runs along
    The thin and sooty river flats
    And stick and straw and random stones
    Steam faintly when its steam departs.

Lime-water and liquorice light
Wander the tumbled streets. A few
Sparrows gather. A dog barks out
Under the dogless pale pale blue.

    Move your tongue along a slat
    Of a raspberry box from last year's crate
    Smell saucepantilt of water
    On the coal-ash in your grate.

Think how the Black Death made men dance,
And from the silt of centuries
The proof is now scraped bare that once
Troy fell and Pompey scorched and froze.

    A boy alone out in the court
    Whacks with his hockey-stick, and whacks
    In the wet, and pigeons flutter, and rise,
    And settle back.

To A Sad Daughter

Michael Ondaatje

All night long the hockey pictures
gaze down at you
sleeping in your tracksuit.
Belligerent goalies are your ideal.
Threats of being traded
cuts and wounds
—all this pleases you.
O my god! You say at breakfast
reading the sports page over the Alpen
as another player breaks his ankle
or assaults the coach.

When I thought of daughters
I wasn't expecting this
but I like this more.
I like all your faults
even your purple moods
when you retreat from everyone
to sit in bed under a quilt.
And when I say "like"
I mean of course "love"
but that embarrasses you.
You who feel superior to black and white movies
(coaxed for hours to see *Casablanca*)
though you were moved
by *Creature from the Black Lagoon.*

One day I'll come swimming
beside your ship or someone will
and if you hear the siren
listen to it. For if you close your ears
only nothing happens. You will never change.
I don't care if you risk
your life to angry goalies
creatures with webbed feet.
You can enter their caves and castles
their glass laboratories. Just
don't be fooled by anyone but yourself.

This is the first lecture I've given you.
You're "sweet sixteen" you said.
I'd rather be your closet friend
than your father. I'm not good at advice
you know that, but ride
the ceremonies
until they grow dark.

Sometimes you are so busy
discovering your friends
I ache with a loss
—but that is greed.
and sometimes I've gone
into *my* purple world
and lost you.

One afternoon I stepped
into your room. You were sitting
at the desk where I now write this.
Forsythia outside the window
and sun spilled over you
like a thick yellow miracle
as if another planet
was coaxing you out of the house
—all those possible worlds!—
and you, meanwhile, busy with mathematics.

I cannot look at forsythia now
without loss, or joy for you.
You step delicately
into the wild world
and your real prize will be
the frantic search.
Want everything. If you break
break going out not in.
How you live your life I don't care
but I'll sell my arms for you,
hold your secrets forever.

If I speak of death
which you fear now, greatly,
it is without answers,
except that each
one we know is
in our blood.
Don't recall graves.
Memory is permanent.
Remember the afternoon's
yellow suburban annunciation.
Your goalie
in his frightening mask
dreams perhaps
of gentleness.

A Stitch in Time
Birk Sproxton

1 The scars tell the story. Nicks and cuts scratched into flesh, worms buried and burrowing under the hide. My hide is an open book. The first chapter starts on my chin, one and one-quarter inches long, one inch below the lower lip, tilting downward a little to the left, from a butt end in the deep slot. Fourteen stitches I snipped off one week later in Winnipeg, 1957. "You should get that looked at right away," said Red, hands on my face. "It's a deep cut. You need stitches, you'll have to shave around it when you get older if you don't get it stitched up right away."

2 And the one you don't see, the secret chapter, runic, hidden behind the right ear. Delivered by skate, the Main Arena, Flin Flon. A red letter day. Some guys don't skate very well. If you lift your heels you lose speed. Somehow his skate met my head. At the company hospital they put a plug in. You can feel it with your fingers. Run your fingers through my hair.

3 Sutures are called catgut, a tough cord made from sheep's intestines. Sutures = catgut = sheepgut. To gut: to hack and slash with a very sharp knife, in the gutting shed. To eviscerate. To fillet. You can do it with a spear. Cut his guts out, like a butcher.

I haven't told anybody this, but the scars embarrass me. That catgut all over your body gets to you after a while, makes you sheepish.

4 Those cuts that haven't been sewn just grow together, stick themselves lip to lip, texture for the tissue. Right thigh, about five inches away from doing real damage, a stray skate, heels lower to the ice. A scar about one inch long, a divot. Just below the left thumb, a v-shape, or maybe an L, the long side about one inch long, fist through a pane of glass early one morning, during a party. She kissed me under the chin. She came along to be my party doll.

Tooth, lower jaw, chipped. Al caught me in the middle of a slap shot, I was watching the puck. O how I love to shoot. You stride over the blue line and line up your body and glide forward, driving with your shoulders, puck in front, waiting for the kick of stick in the ass, embracing twine. Boom Boom Geoffrion strikes again.

5 On newly flooded ice, accelerating skater leaves a string
of oblique stitch marks.

/
\
/
\
/
\
/

       The strides open the ice, cut after cut. In typewriting you
call it a slash. Emily speaks of telling the story slant, she knows
how to sing the ice, sign the ayes, the eyes.

HOME ICE ADVANTAGE

UNIVERSITY
OF
SASKATCHEWA
HOCKEY TEAM
1911 — 1912

F. MacPherson.
P. Peters. (capt:)
R.C. Mitchell.
D.S. MacMurchy
J.R. Bunn.
F.A. Consay.
A.M. Walker.

Higher learning pucksters. (Saskatoon Public Library-Local History Room. Photograph LH3898)

First Blood, 1950
Birk Sproxton

Unused to the new zippered style, the hockey fan catches himself up, short, draws blood, seeks help howling from his giggling sister. Two hands are not enough. He maketh a storm, he prayeth devoutly for buttons, he contemplateth religious conversion.

The street is his first rink, and later he skates with brothers and sisters on the ice of the lake. A fire burns black and sweet inside an old tire. This is the hot tire league. He gathers sticks from the bush beside the tracks, clumps of dead grass from the shoreline.

The lake isn't theirs but the rink is. It parks right beside their garden (a potato garden mainly, big flat rock in the middle, some turnips and cabbages) and they have more kids than the other families, a fruitful bunch—Merle and Gwen and Carol and Wayne and him, the brat they say, and Allen at home with Mom waiting his turn and waiting for Cheryl, the baby of them all—so the rink is theirs twice over. On that rink they skate and skate, and stump home through clenched teeth for Dad to rub their piggies warm, rub them with snow to warm them, his soft black eyes warm through the tears. And next day they go over the banked rocks and through wind and snow to skate again on the lake, their blades rasp, rasping on the ice.

On that lake there are always other rinks—one under the trestle, two or three down at Mile 84, at least two near the Island and God knows how many on the Ross Lake side. And that's only one lake. Uptown there's Hapnot Lake, Schist Lake at Channing, Flin Flon Lake in Creighton. The rink near the Creek Bridge in Lakeside. Ponds and sloughs and ditches and gravel pits. Lots of rinks and plenty of winter.

One year the lake freezes over with no snow cover. The boundaries gone he chases the puck for miles, wind in his chest, the ice slick as glass, crystal clicking, blade cutting. On the rhythmic singing of the ice the puck slides and slides and slides. On that singing lake in the bristle of wind you can push and stride, in the streaming cold, you can stretch out and skate and you do.

Behind the Red Brick House

Charlottetown, P.E.I. 1955
Hugh MacDonald

Doctor Joe and Colin
and the twins
stand in soggy sleeves
behind the house
They lay the water down
in shining pools
night after night
and on frost crisp mornings
break up shells
of tinkle ice
that mar the thickening surface
then melt it down
with steaming floods
and leave for the office and school
impatient for the work to end

Soon come nights
when hordes of children
shove inside the changing shed
fill lungs with kerosene charged air
or sit and wheeze
and tie their skates
on ice-lump mounds
along the edge

Captains toss
an out-of-season bat
pick shouting teams
and nets are coats
or hunk of snow

With eyes like young owls
we stick handle
around figure-skating girls
and flirting pairs
"no lifties" is the rule
but pucks still fly
we scramble over banks
and mine mounds of drift

We play till toes are trapped
laces locked in hanging icicles
We're never more awake
than when we leave
and crunch along the streets
sticks across shoulders
hobo style
our skates
lace-hung and steaming
at our backs
and once in bed
we sleep so fast
and dream
of how we'll play
the next game
and the next

Family Pond
Florence McNeil

On the ice generations twist and writhe
small boys lash their Christmas pucks
and gallop relentlessly away from parents
agonizing
near the snowy borders
of the pond
Grandparents
conscious of the semi-circle
of stares
move in smaller and smaller arcs
and are lost to view
At this perfect moment
we emerge
clear anomalies
mysteriously shearing the ice
in no predestined
direction
oblivious of any need
to race
or cling
warmed by eyes and hands blossoming
unhampered
in a winter
we are only gliding over.

When I Was a Boy and the Farm Pond Froze
John B. Lee

When I was a boy
once every winter the farm pond froze
wide as a field from fence to fence
we'd go down with skates, puck and stick
and play in the burning wind for days
the ice slithering with cracks
under our weight
seeping at first with water, then
collapsing in dried hollows where the furrows
cut tiny valleys
in the plough-rolled earth
till the game shrunk to such boundaries
of ruin
we could hardly turn between the evaporating kingdoms
of snow-boot goals.
Then one terrible day the whole wreckage
broken on the knuckles of frosted clods
would lie fallen like a puzzle tossed in the air.
That was the last of the generous mornings.
The last of the pond
groaning like a fat man's bed
when the wind turned suddenly cold and ordinary
and the snow scattered in filthy patches
stippled with dust.

Ice Time
Ken Rivard

cutting across a park in late November
I stop,
hear voices coming from the bottom
of an empty swimming pool.
a group of boys are playing hockey
with the yellow of a tennis ball.
I don't disturb them.
imagine, playing ball hockey
on the floor of an autumn pool.
the boys are warming up
taking shots from the shallow end
to the deep end.
goaltender finds it easier that way
and
he is using school bags for goalposts.
now that makes sense.
he is letting his friends learn
to put homework
where it should be,
in the middle
of an almost November dark.

At the arena
Kelley Jo Burke

there is
fluorescence
stale popcorn
wood scarred by skate blades healed by falling beer
it's so ugly and cold and
familiar

the guys
horning their lust and rage
offer smokes to the snow maidens
cold-eyed at seventeen
who smile hiding their teeth
and turn back to the game

screams cut the lutheran air

when everyone leaves
even the Zamboni man
when the unforgiving lights are finally down
and the ice is again virginal

skate out in the vaulting
dark

race and turn
like the great ones

the rafters reverberate with
your name
unassisted

the scoreboard shows
that Home has finally won

Classic City Arena on Friday Nights
Barry Butson

The cold walk to the rink,
the warm lobby where
big men in thick red coats
and women in furs are crowded
in talk and smoke, drinking
hot chocolate from paper cups
they crush with heels afterwards,
as they head in for the game.

I am merging with them quite happily
as they pass through the ticket gate,
racing up the stairs
before the ticket-taker can grab me.
Possibly he didn't care;
maybe he grinned.

Cold along the upper level walkway,
standing room only,
players circling the ice
in pre-game ritual I can't see
but can hear the blades slicing
and the pucks being slapped.
I am climbing onto the steel rafters
because there are no empty seats.

An usher may or may not order me down.
Warm by the third period,
temperatures raised by 3,000 fans,
their passion reaching the cold steel rafters
where I perch less like vulture than
one of the swifts that live in the arena's
upper reaches, back pressed against a post
          legs hanging down.

Our team seldom lost
with that Roth, Flick, Flanagan line.
I had no money,
but I saw every game.

Arena

—for Maurice Richard
Don Gutteridge

For the fifteen seasons
of my boyhood
I watched you
in that arena contained
by the TV screen
and the restless cameras
and yet made grander
by them
(like the forests to the north
of our village, with wolves,
like the prairies out West
bristling with Indians
or like the Lake beside us
wider than sea and more salty)
made it grander than our
home-built local rink,
and you, Maurice Richard,
outdistancing
    cameras
    focus
    Maple Leafs
    imagination
carrying my boyhood
on blades
farther than it deserved,
beyond the range
of ice

And when you fell
and your five hundred goals
about you
and the Forum diminished,
I was with you
when the ice gave way
in broken perfect circles,
when the marble timbers
and columns
of our mutual imagination
collapsed
in Roman ruin.

Rink

Joan Finnigan

Yes my grandchildren, when he was born,
a Blue Baby in the fabulous Twenties,
the heart specialist removed his stethoscope
from the tiny, pale, heaving chest,
pronounced to the suspended parents,
"This little lad will never play hockey.
An enlarged heart. Perhaps six months—."

Out of Ottawa and into the pure clear air
of the Upper Pontiac, she and her mother,
with all the old-time rural remedies,
breathed into the child the breath of life,
love, stronger than the inchoate heart
of primitive stars,
belief, deeper than cosmic infinity,
refusing death's entry.

Just to prove that doctors
are not really gods,
he was on the backyard rink
by age three, double-edged skates
and miniature hockey sticks, custom-forged
in his father's national arena of glory,
the old Ottawa Senators' Auditorium.

His undauntable damaged heart
would not let him play fast forward,
but his great eyes and genetic reflexes
marked out for him his permanent place
in goal.

Road hockey, pond hockey, pick-up hockey,
river hockey, backyard hockey,
in simulation of his All-Star father,
he played his time-bomb heart
into the local annals of courage,
when Glashan rink gates were locked
even climbed the chain-link fence,
fifteen feet high,
with his skates on,
to join the pick-up team
on Saturday mornings.

Stood at night with his ear lugs down,
thirty below zero, hose in hand,
swinging smooth, steady waters
onto the perennial backyard rink
at his own house, no girls allowed
to scratch and mess up the ice, soften the atmosphere

Dedicated, determined, pig-headed
like his father and fathers before him,
as his enlarging heart grew
it humped his teenage back,
but augmented his courage,
so sorely needed when his younger brother
went on to join the ranks of Junior A

In the wartime Forties,
still rejecting his destiny,
to be closer to the game he adored
(and the faltering father
he still worshipped)
he moved to a wider rink,
up and down the stairs
of the old Ottawa Auditorium,
(his faulty heart working hard,
fighting gravity) where he sold
hockey programmes while his father
scored on the ice below
for an ailing Air Force Team

When he died at age thirty
in the arms of the old hockey player,
right above Canada
God made the first rink in heaven
put up golden goal-posts,
blew the opening whistle
on an eternal hockey game.

WINNERS AND LOSERS

The renowned Ottawa Hockey Club "Silver Seven," winners of the 1905 Stanley Cup.

The Hockey Player Sonnets
—for Al Purdy
John B. Lee

i

What about them Leafs, eh!
(expletive deleted*) couldn't score an (e.d.) goal
if they propped the (e.d.'s)up
in front of the (e.d.) net
and put the (e.d.) puck on their (e.d.) stick
and the (e.d.) goalie fell asleep
and somebody (e.d.) yelled, 'SHOOT THE (e.d.) THING!'
 (E-E-E-E. D-eeeeeee!!!!!!!!)

ii

(e.d.)!! this (e.d.) shower's (e.d.)cold.
who the (e.d.) flushed the (e.d.) toilet?
give me the (e.d.) soap.
hand me that (e.d.) towel.
has anybody got some (e.d.) shampoo.
toss the (e.d.) over here!
thanks. what's this (e.d.) pansy (e.d.)?

who brought the (e.d.) beer?
toss me one. stop throwing that (e.d.) snow.
you could lose an (e.d.) eye.
and so on ...

iii

What do you mean you don't watch sports on TV.
Why the (e.d.) not?
Haven't you got an (e.d.) TV?
What the (e.d.) do you watch?
What the (e.d.) do you do?

Read! ! !—who the (e.d.) wants to (e.d.) read!
too much like (e.d) thinkin'.

there is much (e.d.) laughter at this.
and so it goes—
'what about them Leafs, eh ...'

hereinafter referred to as 'e.d.'

68

Dragging Buses With Your Teeth

—For Stéphane
C.H. (Marty) Gervais

The only thing
I was good at
was table hockey
and there was a time
when I'd retreat to
the backroom of the
newspaper bureau
and play the guys
in circulation
and make them buy me lunch
but I was terrible
on the ice, couldn't
stand up on my skates
couldn't score a goal
even if there was
an open net and pylons
directing the way to the net
I'd screw it up somehow
and last night
when I got off the phone
with a scout from Montana
who's looking at signing
my second oldest son
I wondered about it all
For years I've been standing
behind the glass
at the boards watching my boys cutting
across the ice
their eyes fixed
on the puck
their bodies as swift
and clean and graceful
as a hawk above
a morning meadow
I wonder about it
where they learned this
where they found
that inherent
skill that natural
beauty that way
about them as they
float before a goalie
with all the confidence

of a magician playing
out a slight of hand
It couldn't be me
There were no Gervais
of any great hockey
talent, hell, sports
ability—except one
a guy from Montreal
Who in the '50s could
pull buses with his teeth
—if you call that sports
He'd strut out on
St. Catherine Street
clad only in a bathing suit
and he'd strap a rope
or wire of some kind
to the front of the bus
and use a special mouth
piece and slowly
with businessmen, housewives
and kids crowding him
would gently move
this lumbering old bus
along the street
That's it
—the rest of us
all failures when it
comes to pucks or baseballs
or tennis rackets or
swimming or anything
We were good with
words—grandsons of
a liar, sons of an
inventor and we wound up
selling shoes, insurance
became writers or priests
or telephone solicitors
made our living
with words, trotting out
Truth and Glory and Greatness
making people believe
the unbelievable

Anecdote of the Hockey Game
Gerald Hill

When a twelve-year-old boy, early for his ice time,
enters Dressing Room 8, picks a spot
to dump his equipment and sit down
while the old-timers pack up and leave,
a man named Roger, number 27, a man from Saskatchewan,
takes the opportunity to speak to the boy. *I'll tell you
a few things* he says. *Listen.*

Out on the ice the kid plays quieter than usual,
can't get him to say a single word, can't see
where he is. Sometimes you hear
his skates, behind, then ahead. The kid
skates for miles, doesn't mind darkness
or light, doesn't mind what gets in his way,
the masked faces, the red and blue lines.
He never gets where he's going but is always there,
looking for the loose puck, driving it home.

Toward the end of the third period with the game at its darkest,
he breaks across the blue line, no one
from him to the goalie, infinite time
to settle inside his next few moves. He breaks
in alone and lights up the red light just like
the man from Saskatchewan told him.

Summer Hockey Camp

Donna Kane

outside it's forty-four above
the sun swollen and heavy
as the fruit being sold
along the highway to the arena
From the bleachers of the hockey rink
we watch out children in their skates and hockey pads
our breath levelling in air that feels of melting ice-cream
the coach drops a bucket of pucks
and they scatter across the ice like watermelon seeds
In an indefinite sensible space
everything is forgiven
the soft outline
of my daughter's face
her body moving across the ice
as easily as any boy's

The B-P-T
Gary Hyland

Two 3's fixed on the scoreboard,
two minutes left, last game of the finals.
I pick up a rebound beside our net, spot
our centre breaking, bank one off the boards
which their winger takes in stride and slaps
hard and high into our net for the winner.

Half an hour later, most of the guys gone,
I'm still in skates when Gord, the coach,
taps my ankle, mutters, "B-P-T,"
and slouches from the dressing room.

I swore not to return for the next season
but I loved the game and managed to con
myself into believing I'd improved enough
to be considered average and wouldn't puke
before, after or during games. My decision
brought out the sadist in Gord. One night
he explains the B-P-T to the whole team.

"Sports doctors found some players panic
at key times. Seize right up, make dumbass
plays. Turns out they found theses guys got
a special anatomical quirk—a super long
tendon connecting their right ankle bone
to this bit of brain they try to think with."
The bugger keeps glancing right at me.
"Under pressure, this tendon tightens,
so when they moved their legs their brains
disconnect. That's the Brain Pulling Tendon,
B-P-T for short." The guys have a snigger.

I knew he was right. Except it was an ocean
of adrenalin drowning a speck of confidence
that shot me into chaos or paralysis, not
some freak tendon. Same difference though.

That year's big game is the season ender
a playoff-qualifier against the Hawks
and the score's one all with me benched
the last ten minutes till Fraz gets pretzled
on their goal post and Hooey is ousted
trying to nag a penalty call. There's maybe
a minute left when I hit the ice stiff and cold
and right away I'm in trouble because Metcalf,
their hotshot, is breaking down the far side,
not my wing but I'm the only one with a chance
to catch him. My legs are moving like I'm
hauling bricks on butter, my eyes are blurred.

As Metcalf pulls away I'm actually thinking,
"Gord, you prick, thanks for this B-P-T."
But Metcalf must have got one himself.
He spins out of control trying to deke me.
Me who couldn't have checked his shadow.
I grab the loose puck and wonder how
I'm going to botch this one as two forwards
swarm in. Desperate, I dump the puck
between them and, holy sheepshit, Midge,
our centre, nabs it and flips a perfect pass
to Massey who whacks it home for the win.

Am I a hero? Me who scared Metcalf puckless
and bank-rolled the game-winning goal?
Does the Pope get cards on Father's Day?
The score sheet reads Massey from Mijewski,
Gord ignores me in his post-game kudos,
Massey and Metcalf last a few go-rounds
in the NHL, and I grunt each year in no-hit
still barfing, still trying to tame my B-P-T.

The Song of the Stay-at-Home Defenceman

Birk Sproxton

The last time I tried to score I got knocked ass over tea kettle at the blue line and they broke in on a two-on-one and tied the game. The coach yelled at me, called me a big lug, tugged me by the forelock. Screamed so loud he got a hernia. I got sent down for two weeks.

Don't send you to the minors, those guys, they send you to the mines. You work, underground, in the miner leagues. You come out looking like a mole, you get dirty pores and gauchies, your eyes grow about two inches wider from squinting in the shadows. And hot. You get closer to hell and it heats up. Yaaaaah, heats up as you go down.

> *Other guys fool around, tool around*
> *Even dipsydoo'le around*
> *I got the lowdown, way down*
> *Stay-at-home defenceman shoes.*

You have to be there, you can't hot dog about, streak with the wingers, deke everybody out of their underwear, scoring all the time. You have to suck it up and hang in. Protect things. Stay home and look after the crease. Take the banging and whacking, lay a few good whacks yourself.

> *You don't fool around, tool around*
> *Got to keep your cool around*
> *The hometown, showdown*
> *Stay-at-home defenceman dues.*

Other guys get the fun. You've got responsibilities. Keep them out of the slot, out of the crease. That's what you're there for. Keep it clean in front.

> *Other guys fool around, tool around*
> *Even dipsydoo'le around*
> *I got the stay put*
> *Lowdown leadfoot*
> *Stay-at-home defenceman*
> *Won't let me play around*
> *The lowdown deadfoot*
> *Stay-at-home defenceman*
> *Blooooooooooze.*

And then one fall the CNR Dayliner, a speedy passenger train takes him to The Pas, and the old milk train to yellow rooms in the Winnipeg YMCA, cheap restaurants, the Winnipeg Braves, the St. Boniface Canadiens exhibiting themselves in Flin Flon, the United College Redmen, and then west and south by bus now to the Boissevain Border Kings, and later, west again to play left wing for a literary magazine in Regina (the magazine is The Sphinx, the people Sphinxters, the hockey team the Obfuskaters), then back to Winnipeg where he breaks retirement to play for the graduate students against the English profs the year before Al Purdy is there to write a poem about the game, and west again, bang up against the cowboy Rockies to Red Deer and the Big Belly No Hit League, the NHL at last.

As a parent he travels again, over the Rocks into B.C., across Alberta, Saskatchewan, Manitoba, to Ontario, to Europe. By telephone to Quebec and British Columbia, Washington and Oregon, Germany and Czechoslovakia. Always on the road, ride, riding.

The Mintos, the little yellow sweater with a cloverleaf, Champs 1950–51. The Kinsmen, blue and gold. The Doghouse, yes, blue with red and white, sponsored by the local teenage hotdog and hamburger hangout, fries with gravy, Flin Flon Juvenile Champs, 1959–60. The Rink Rats. The Flin Flon Midget Bombers, Manitoba Midget A Champs, 1959–60, maroon and white. The Winnipeg Braves, black and orange. The St. Boniface Canadiens, a Christmas exhibition game against Flin Flon, in borrowed skates, le bleu blanc rouge. The United College Redmen, University of Manitoba Inter-Faculty Champs, 1963–64, red and white. The Boissevain Border Kings, gold and black. The Obfuskaters, a motley crew. I bought my first curved hockey stick. Mark and I played on the outdoor rink, he got away on me, walked on the snowy crusts across the park. The Red Deer College Big Bellies, gold with black, stretched.

Once Is Once Too Many
Stephen Scriver

I only forgot to wear my can
once   that was enough

it was one time over in Glenavon
I went out for my first shift
and you know how when you're waiting
for the drop of the puck
you lean over and rest
your stick across your can
well, this time all I can feel
is wide-open spaces and the family jewels

but I'm not gonna skate
back to the bench
so I figger I'll get by
for this shift anyways

well, I'm all over the ice
like a mad man's shit and
I chase the puck into their corner
pass it back to Brian on defence
then head for the net to screen the goalie

when I look back to the point
sure as God's got sandals
Brian's just blasted one crotch-high

Not to worry I figger
I'll just jump and let it cruise
between my legs

well, I couldn'ta timed'er
more perfect   it was just
like a three-ball combination

cept that two of them were damn
near in my throat
while the puck caroms into the net
like snot off a door knob

was I pleased?
is the Pope married?

Goin Down

Stephen Scriver

Yer not playin with a full deck
if you go down to block a shot
in this kinda hockey—
take Dickie there   did it once too often
and hasn't laced on a skate since

It was the '72 playoffs
the Monarchs had a power play
and Latourneau winds up at the point
with a shot so hard
he damn near tears out his arsehole

Well, Dickie goes down to block
And for a second there's no puck
till he spits it out
right on the blue line
with about a dozen teeth

Latourneau?   Hell, he takes that puck
stick-handles through them teeth and scores
while we stand there crotch-bound
like a buncha decoys

Dickie? Well, he never was much
to look at anyways

Canadian Angels

Lorna Crozier

—(written for our women's hockey team at the Olympics for the final against the
   Americans, February 21, 2002)

Angels of the House, Angels of Mercy—yes, they've called women that. But these
are Angels of Ice. Hard-muscled, sharp, dangerous as winter's cold. How else do
you explain their speed, the light streaming from their helmets, the slivers of water
under their burning blades that cut across the blue lines like scissors slicing through
the cotton for a quilt?

Lace to these gals is lacing up. Cinnamon and allspice is slapshot, snapshot,
backhand, wrist—that's the recipe they're passing on from mothers to daughters, to
women like me whose brothers in our races at outdoor rinks, skated backwards and
beat us every time.

Break away, break away, swift angels carrying the puck, invisible wings beating,
your goalie a blaze of glory in the crease.

All across the North we'll roar and cheer. You'll fly us far above the boards, above
the rooftop of the rink tonight, fly us into the skate-blade brightness of the winter
stars.

Rhéaume

Richard Harrison

Here is the desire of Manon Rhéaume: to stop
the puck. Come down from the stands, strap on the big
pads, painted mask, disappear into *goalie* the way
a man can be a man and not a man inside the
armour. To forget in the motion of the save that we
do not forget she is always a woman and sex is
everything: if she wasn't pretty she'd never hear her
looks got her on the NHL team in Tampa Bay
where the ushers are women hired from a bar
called *Hooters,* and David Letterman wouldn't have
her on *Late Night* prodding her again and again, *Say
Ock-ee;* if Brett Hull was ugly as a wet owl and
scored 86 goals a season, still there'd be kids with
his poster on their bedroom doors. To be a woman
and have it be her play that counts. To stop the
puck where the best are men, for men to be better
than they are. On your wall is a collage of women
with their arms raised, they are dancing, they are
lifting weights, they are marching against apartheid.
One is a goddess with snakes in her hands;
Catwoman reaches for Gotham, Boadicea shakes a
spear in the face of Rome, two nuns run splashing
into the laughing waves: here, I give you Rhéaume
and a glove save, the puck heading for the top
corner. Stopped.

The Ballad of Wendel Clark
The Rheostatics

Part 1
Martin Tielli
Part 11
Dave Clark and Dave Bidini

Part I
Got a friend in BC, know some winders kissing New York.
And I wanna buy a motorcycle and cut up to some farm …

Somewhere in this cowshit county, where the hills are round and green …

Late nights make me really tired, all this jamming gives me a headache.
Like listening to earthquakes all wired up for rock and roll.
Mama only listens to the radio.
Papa only watches hockey games.
This suburb rocks with the Eddie Van Wailers.
God save the Queen—she made you a moron!

Part II
Well I heard Wendel talking to Dave Hodge last night –
And he said that he was confident and keen.
And he said that Jacques Plante didn't die
So all of us could glide,
He said that hard work is the ethic of the free.

Wendel was a man with a stick in his hands
Who learned how to play in Kelvington, S-A-S-K.
You'll wish that you had died,
When Wendel has your hide,
'Cause he does it the Canadian way.

So now we sit around on the couch and watch TV
And we see Wendel leading the team.
Well, if God made Clark on the seventh day,
He knew what He was doing if He did.
(If He did!)

Wendel was a man with a stick in his hands
Who learned how to play in Kelvington, S-A-S-K.
You'll wish that you had died,
When Wendel has your hide,
'Cause he does it the Canadian way.

Like this: Bam, Bam—digga digga damm!
Clear the trap, 'cause here comes Wendel.
Number seventeen, I mean it!

Wendel was a man with a stick in his hands
Who learned how to play in Kelvington, S-A-S-K.
You'll wish that you had died,
When Wendel has your hide,
'Cause he does it the Canadian way.

To an Athlete Dying Young

A.E. Housman

The time you won your town the race
We chaired you through the market-place;
Man and boy stood cheering by,
And home we brought you shoulder-high.

To-day, the road all runners come,
Shoulder-high we bring you home,
And set you at your threshold down,
Townsman of a stiller town.

Smart lad, to slip betimes away
From fields where glory does not stay
And early though the laurel grows
It withers quicker than the rose.

Eyes the shady night has shut,
Cannot see the record cut,
And silence sounds no worse than cheers
After earth has stopped the ears:

Now you will not swell the rout
Of lads that wore their honours out,
Runners whom renown outran
And the name died before the man.

So set, before its echoes fade,
The fleet foot on the sill of shade,
And hold to the low lintel up
The still-defended challenge-cup.

And round that early-laurelled head
Will flock to gaze the strengthless dead,
And find unwhithered on its curls
The garland briefer than a girl's.

Fifty Mission Cap
The Tragically Hip

Bill Barilko disappeared
that summer
He was on a fishing trip
The last goal he ever scored
won the Leafs the cup
They didn't win another
'til 1962
the year he was discovered
I stole this from a hockey card
I keep tucked up under

My Fifty Mission Cap
I worked it in
to look like that

Bill Barilko disappeared
that summer (in 1950)
He was on a fishing trip (in a plane)
The last goal he ever scored (in overtime)
won the Leafs the cup
They didn't win another
'til 1962
The year he was discovered

My Fifty Mission Cap
I worked it in
to look like that

Dying on the Ice at 39 is Hard
John B. Lee

He stepped onto the ice
circled twice
fell flat   and died.

No Shakesperean monologues.
No dying words for a desperate son.
No pyrotechnics of the heart.
It just suddenly stopped
like a small bird slamming into glass.

His teammates gathered
in a stunned huddle
then breathed away from him
on worried skates
that day they tore their calendars
like grieving widows.

He went cold so fast
his pulse stuck on the half beat
like a swirling coin under a gambler's thumb
and he lay in a limp heap.

Whether November moves in the bones of a tree
or April is coral coloured with crocus
sea-shelled in a tiny garden
death comes when death comes
and 'he was dead when he hit the ice'
but lying on the ice at 39 is hard.

On the busride home
they carried his corpse
in the beer cooler
and drank quietly
like buck-deer in a moonlit clearing
thinking about what everyone who has ever lived
is too stupid to understand.

Fogarty
Richard Harrison

Tell me to fuck off, you'd be right; I know nothing
of what it's like to be the most celebrated defence-
man in junior, to roll under your skates the recorded
legacy of Bobby Orr, to be photographed with my
stick *on fire* I was that hot at—what was it?—18?
19?—I can't remember, to become the rushing
defenceman stepfather of four kids and just out of
school—straight A's—wanting and wanting so much
to be a man, anchor the rush on the sloppiest defence
of the weakest team in the League—you love them,
they are yours. The shots pour by anyway. All year
I wrote home I was happy, I said, so glad to be
chosen. I do not know what's left that's true.
I couldn't answer even the most basic question;
When did you know you were a defenceman? I mean,
you must have believed in yourself when no one else
did, and now you want to be anywhere but there,
taking the face-off in the middle of the ring of a
drink poured carelessly, spilled over ice.

Johnny
Stephen Scriver

Even in my boozed-up glow
the old drunk offends me
barging into our table
in Rouleau pub coughing
an picking up a draught

he looks away from my scowl
to my jacket
Grenfell Hockey Club eh?
Yknow I played for P.A. Mintos 34 ta 36

I smirk into my glass
then look at my buddy
Sure   Old hockey players don't die
They just lose their cans
but he's not laughing

the old guy coughs and goes on
Yep had a shot at the Leafs in 37
I cough a mouthful
and look at my buddy who sez
Show him the clippings Johnny

and he lifts a pouch
from his Sally Ann coat
and pushes it at me

and I read
"Gervais Scores Four in Playoff Romp ...
speedy little centreman ...
sensational stickhandling display ...
scouts from the NHL ..."

and I look from words to man
and back to words
till my hesitant eyes get him going

primed on free beer
he's really into it
how the stick in his hands charmed the puck
how the goalies he deked could fill a stadium
and how the booze and bad lungs got to him
before he laced on those big-time skates

an I can only listen and pay
wonder if some day I'll need free beer

Grey is the Forelock Now of the Irishman
Joan Finnigan

Grey is the forelock now of the Irishman,
stick-handler of my roaring Twenties birthright,
F. Scott Fitzgerald of the sporting world,
(and, between games, father to me).

My beautiful brain-washed Canadian sons
are bringing in the whole neighbourhood
to see the old pro alive,
the all-round right-wing Maple Leaf god,
Adonis of an arena now crumbled
and fallen into the cannibal maw of mobs.

The boys, crowding in at the door,
surround him with a fiery ring of worship,
envying his eyebrows,
thick with scars inflicted by the high sticking
of old idols, Clancy, Morenz, Horner—

(and, my god, one of them is standing at attention!)

When I was their age, unholily dreamful,
full of the same power of innocence,
I saw crowds pick him up and carry him away,
policemen trampled down,
hysterical women following their infatuation
to the barricaded hotel-room doors,
crying in the corridors
their need for illusion;

and I remember the millionaires who courted him
whose money had not brought them youth
and the golden skates of fame;
one of them especially used to invite him
into his suite at the Royal York for an oyster feed,
then ordered up by phone,
crustaceans, wine, stove, pans, chef and all;
another used to send him every Christmas
suitably engraved silver dishes
which my mother never used;

I remember my father, too, in the headlines,
on the gum cards, in the rotogravure,
and how, in the pasture, there was nothing
to charge but shadows and, in the dark beyond night,
bright enormous butterflies crossing the moon
of his disenchanted vision; I heard him cry out to them
in another room but they stayed in his eyes
until we were all well-marked by the days
of his going down into ruin.

Wrinkled now is the brow of my all-star father
standing in the doorway
of the house of his grandsons
who yet must learn,
in smaller forums and with less limelight,
how heroes are really made.

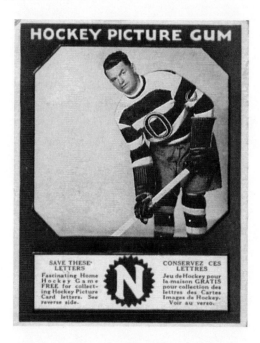

Front and back of Canadian Chewing Gum hockey
card. (Courtesy of Michael P.J. Kennedy)

FRANK FINNIGAN
Ottawa Senators

Played Senior Amateur Hockey with Monta-grads Club. Signed by Senators in 1924. Made good from the start, and has been with Ottawa except for 1931-32 season when he was on loan to Toronto Maple Leafs.

Joua du Senior Amateur Hockey avec le Club Montagrads. Engagé par les Sénateurs en 1924. Brilla dès le début, et a toujours été avec Ottawa excepté en 1931-32 lorsqu'il fut prêté aux Maple Leafs de Toronto.

For collecting sufficient correct letters to spell the full names of any 5 of the following teams we will mail FREE a Home Hockey Game.

Pour la collection des lettres épelant en entier 5 des équipes suivantes, nous enverrons GRATIS un Jeu de Hockey pour la Maison.

Toronto Maple Leafs, Montreal Cana-diens, New York Rangers, Ottawa Sena-tors, Chicago Black Hawks, Boston Bruins, Detroit Red Wings, Montreal Maroons, New York Americans.

(Names of teams must be spelled out in full as listed)
(Les noms doivent être épelés comme sur la liste)

Mention 5 teams and letters you are sending in when returning to

Mentionnez les 5 équipes et les lettres en les retournant à:

CANADIAN CHEWING GUM SALES LTD.
Dept. A-1, 14 Dickens St., Toronto 8, Ont.

Roster of Authors

THE ARROGANT WORMS consisting of Chris Patterson (bass & vocals), Trevor Strong (vocals), and Mike McCormick (guitar & vocals) are originally from Kingston, Ontario. Their albums include: *The Arrogant Worms* (1992), *Russell's Shorts* (1994), *C'est Cheese* (1995), *Live Bait* (1997), *Christmas Turkey* (1997), *Dirt* (1999), *Idiot Road* (2001), *Gift Wrapped* (2002), *Semi-Conducted* (2003), and *Toast* (2004).

MARGARET AVISON, the youngest of two daughters of a Methodist minister and his wife, was born in Galt, Ontario in 1918. She spent her childhood in Regina and Calgary before the family moved to Toronto in 1929. She wrote poetry at an early age and one of her poems was published in the children's page of the *Calgary Herald* in 1925 when she was seven years old. In high school, some of her work was published under the pseudonym of Willamac, and others under her own name Margaret Kirkland. At Victoria College of University of Toronto her work appeared in *Acta Victoriana*. In 1956-57 she dedicated all her efforts to writing after receiving a Guggenheim Memorial Grant. *Winter Sun* appeared in 1960 winning the Governor General's Award for poetry. *The Dumbfounding* was published in 1966, *Sunblue* (which also won the Governor General's Award) in 1978, *No Time* (1989), and *Not Yet But Still* (1997), and *Concrete and Wild Carrot* in 2002 which won The Griffin Prize for Poetry. The Porcupine's Quill is currently working towards a three-volume collection of Avison's poems entitled *Always Now*. Two of the volumes are in print with the third slated to appear in 2005. An Officer of the Order of Canada, Margaret Avison has also received D.Litt. degrees from Acadia and York Universities and doctor of sacred letters from Victoria University.

ROGER BELL was born in Port Elgin, Ontario in 1949 and has B.A. in English and B.Ed. degrees from University of Western Ontario. For twenty-nine years he taught English in Simcoe County before retiring in 2004. His publications include *Mythtakes* (1984), *Luke and the Wolf* (1997), and four more volumes: *Real Lives* (1997), *When the Devil Calls* (2000), *Henry's Creature: Poems and Stories on the Automobile* (2000), and *Larger Than Life* (2002). He is currently working on a novel, a memoir, and perhaps a play. *The Pissing Women of Lafontaine*, a poetry collection, should appear in 2005.

KELLEY JO BURKE is a Regina-based award-winning playwright, poet, director, documentarian, and broadcaster. Born at Westminister, Massachusetts in 1961, Ms. Burke has had her plays produced around the world. *Charming and Rose: True Love* has been produced over thirty times in Canada, the U.S., and Europe. Her radio drama, *Big Ocean*, has been heard in seven different countries. She is a graduate of the Universities of Winnipeg and Regina, and the Manitoba Theatre Workshop. A two-time winner of the City of Regina Writing Award, Kelley Jo Burke was a finalist for both the Dora and Chalmers awards for playwrighting and captured several other honours for her poetry and stage work. Her directing and producing projects for stage and radio have included *The Velvet Devil, Sarah Binks, Unity 1918*, and *My Indian Brother*. She has been a regular contributor to CBC's national and regional current affairs shows including "This Morning," and associate producer of "Ideas," and host/producer of "Gallery."

BARRY BUTSON lives in Woodstock, Ontario and was born in 1941 at Stratford, Ontario where he attended school and played sports, one year earning Minor Athlete of the Year. He received his M.A. in English from University of Western Ontario and became a journalist, and later a high school teacher. He began writing poetry fairly late in life but now has had numerous poems published around the world. His first collection, *East End Poems*, which appeared in 1998, won the Milton Acorn People's Poetry Award. Subsequent collections have been *Black Ice* (2000) and *Patio Life* (2004). He is working on his fourth book entitled *Poems from the Produce Department*.

ROCH CARRIER was born in 1937 at Sainte-Justine-de-Dorchester, Quebec and graduated from College Saint-Louis in New Brunswick and University of Montreal. He earned a doctorate at the Sorbonne in Paris. He has written several novels (including *La Guerre, Yes Sir!* in 1968, *Floralie, Where Are You?* in 1971, *Is It the Sun, Philibert?* in 1970 translated into English in 1972, *They Won't Demolish Me* in 1974, and *The Garden of Delights* in 1978), plays (including *La Guerre, Yes Sir!, La celeste bicyclette*, and *Le cirque noir*), and poems, but is perhaps best known for his short stories, especially those contained in *The Hockey Sweater and Other Stories* which appeared in 1979. He has served as executive director of The Canada Council and as National Librarian for Canada.

NILS CLAUSSON was born in New Westminster, British Columbia in 1946. He received his B.A. and M.A. from Simon Fraser University and a Ph.D. from Dalhousie University. After teaching at several universities in Ontario and Alberta he settled at University of Regina where he continues to teach English. His poetry and fiction have appeared in over a dozen Canadian and American journals. His one-act play *Tess and the Boys* won a national writing contest in 1997 and his poetry has appeared in several anthologies. He has published numerous scholarly articles and is currently working on a book on the theory and practice of genre criticism. He also hopes to expand his one-act play into a full-length drama.

STOMPIN' TOM CONNORS was born in 1936 at Saint John, New Brunswick and raised by a foster family at Skinners Pond. He began writing songs at the age of 11 and spent his teenage years hitchhiking and playing his guitar throughout Canada. His first lengthy engagement was at the Maple Leaf Hotel in Timmins, Ontario. He has written more than 300 songs and recorded over 40 albums which have sold more than 3 million copies. A member of the Order of Canada, he also holds an honourary doctorate of laws degree. A Canadian icon, Connors continues to play at various venues across the country.

LORNA CROZIER currently resides in Victoria where she teaches creative writing. She was born in Swift Current, Saskatchewan in 1948. After receiving a B.A. from University of Saskatchewan, she returned to Swift Current where she taught high school and wrote poetry. She was an active member of the Saskatchewan Writers Guild and contributed to the literary community through classes at Saskatchewan Summer School for the Arts and other Guild-sponsored workshops. *Inside Is The Sky* which appeared in 1976 was her first collection of poetry. It was followed by *Crow's Black Joy* (1978), *Humans and Other Beasts* (1980), *The Garden Going On Without Us* (1985), *Angels of Flesh, Angels of Silence* (1988). Her 1992 collection, *Inventing the Hawk* won the Governor General's Award for Poetry and the Pat Lowther Award. *Everything Arrives at the Light*, which was published in 1995, also captured the Lowther Award. This was followed by her tribute to Sinclair Ross' character in *As For Me And My House*, entitled *A Saving Grace: The Collected Poems of Mrs. Bentley* (1996), and *What the Living Won't Let Go* (1999). With her partner, Patrick Lane, she has edited two collections of young Canadian poets, *Breathing Fire* and *Breathing Fire 2* (2004) and a collection of essays called *Addicted: Notes from the Belly of the Beast* (2001). She has received an honourary doctorate from University of Regina and is a Distinguished Professor at University of Victoria.

KATHLEEN EDWARDS who was born in 1979 in Ottawa, had parents who were in the foreign service and therefore she moved around to different places including Korea and Switzerland. Nevertheless, she was influenced by Canadian musicians Tom Petty and Neil Young along with American Bob Dylan. She began to write songs soon after graduating from high school. She moved from Ottawa to rural Quebec and began assembling material for her first album in 2000. "Hockey Skates" appears on *Failer* which was released in 2002. She currently resides in Toronto and her latest album is entitled *Back To Me*.

JOAN FINNIGAN (MACKENZIE) was born in 1925 and raised in Ottawa. After attending Lisgar Collegiate, she received a B.A. in English and Economics from Queen's University before enrolling at Carleton University where she studied journalism. Her father was Frank Finnigan, the last living member of the original NHL Ottawa Senators team. Joan Finnigan has been a reporter whose work appeared in the Ottawa *Journal* as well as CBC radio and the National Film Board. She wrote the screenplay for the Genie and Etrog-winning *The Best Damn Fiddler from Calabogie to Kaladar*.

Her dozens of publications demonstrate a wide range of interests from oral history to hockey to poetry. Included are poetry collections such as *It Was Warm and Sunny When We Set Out* (1970), *The Watershed Collection* (1992), and *Second Wind, Second Sight* (1998). Fiction and children's literature include *The Dog Who Wouldn't Be Left Behind* (1989), *Witches, Ghosts, and Loups-Garous* (1994), *Dancing at the Crossroads* (1995), and *Down The Unmarked Roads* (1997). Her non-fiction includes *Tell Me Another Story* (1988), *Some of the Stories I Told You Were True* (1981), *Tallying the Tales of the Old Timers* (1999) and *Old Scores, New Goals: The Story of the Ottawa Senators* (1992). Joan Finnigan currently divides her residence between Hartington, Ontario and Aylmer, Quebec. Projects forthcoming include a third collection of short stories, *Along the Roven Line*, a memoir, a love poetry collection, *Looking for a Turn-out: Poetry New and Collected*, and an Ottawa Valley collection of humour.

C.H. MARTY GERVAIS was born in Windsor, Ontario in 1946 and was educated at University of Guelph, where he received a B.A.in English in 1971 and University of Windsor, where he received an M.A. in Creative Writing in 1972. He has worked as a journalist for more than thirty years and is currently a columnist for the Windsor *Star*. His journalism has been recognized with more than two dozen newspaper prizes and his book, *The Rumrunners*, a history of prohibition (1980), sold more than 25,000 copies. A founder of Black Moss Press, he has had more than two dozen volumes of his own poetry, short stories, plays, and children's literature published. Included are *Letters from the Equator* (1986), *Playing God* (1995), *Tearing Into a New Day: Selected Poems* (1996) and *To Be Now: New and Selected Poems* (2003), which captured the Mayor's Award for the City of Windsor. His work has also won the Milton Acorn People's Poetry Award and the Harbourfront Festival Prize.

DON GUTTERIDGE has retired as Professor Emeritus from University of Western Ontario where he has been professor of curriculum studies in the Faculty of Education for many years. Born in Sarnia, Ontario in 1937, Gutteridge grew up in Point Edward, Ontario and later attended University of Western Ontario. His publications include a number of books on curriculum studies and more than twenty volumes of poetry and prose including *Riel* (1968), *Borderlands* (1975), *Tecumseh* (1978), *God's Geography* (1982), *Love in the Wintertime* (1990), *Flute Music in Cello's Belly* (1997), *Bus-Ride* (1974), and *Winter's Descent* (1996). His latest, in the Marc Edwards mystery series, includes *Turncoat* (2003) and *Solumn Vows* (2003). At lease two more await publication. In 2004, he published his *Poems: Something More Miraculous*.

RICHARD HARRISON lives in Calgary where he teaches English and Creative Writing at Mount Royal College. Born in Toronto in 1957, Harrison has also taught at Trent University in Ontario and been an editor for Banff Centre Press and University of Calgary Press, and is a member of the editorial board of Wolsak & Wynn. He received his B.Sc. in Biology and an Honours B.A. in Philosophy from Trent and an M.A. in English from Concordia in Montreal. Harrison won the Harbourfront "Discovery" reading prize in 1978 and the City of Calgary W.O. Mitchell Book Prize in 1999. His poetry collections include *Fathers Never*

Leave You (1987), *Recovering the Naked Man* (1991), *Hero of the Play* (1994), *Big Breath of a Wish* (1999), and *Hero of the Play: 10th Anniversary Edition* (2004), an expanded edition of his popular hockey poetry collection. His *Worthy of His Fall* is to be released in September, 2005. He is also working on a book of essays on hockey and poetry and a second co-authored with Lee Easton on modernism, post-modernism and the graphic novel.

GERRY HILL was born at Herbert, Saskatchewan in 1951. He completed his B.Ed. at University of Calgary, a Diploma in Creative Writing from David Thompson University Centre (1982), and an M.A. in English from University of Alberta in 1990. He has taught at Luther College and Saskatchewan Indian Federated College (First Nations University) at University of Regina since 1996. Prior to that he has taught at Red Deer College, University of Alberta, and community and vocational colleges in Regina, Saskatoon, and Edmonton as well as at secondary institutions. He has done freelance writing for a variety of organizations and his creative writing has appeared in a number of anthologies and periodicals. His own publications include *Getting to Know You* (2003), *The Man From Saskatchewan* (2001), and *Heartwood* (1985). He has won the Saskatchewan Book Award for poetry in 2004, City of Regina Writing Award in 2002, John V. Hicks Manuscript Award in 2000 and the James P. Follinsbee Memorial Award for Creative Writing 1988-89.

A.E. HOUSMAN was born near Bromsgrove, Worcestershire, England in 1859 and died in 1936. He studied Greek and Latin as a boy in school and later attended Oxford where he helped found *Ye Rounde Table* undergraduate magazine of verse and satire. He ultimately earned an M.A. and taught at Bromsgrove School, but lived in poverty until he took a position with the Patent Office in London. While at the Patent Office, he spent much of his non-working time studying the classics and writing commentaries on classical works. Most of his own poetry was not published until after his death. His 1886 *A Shropshire Lad* was one of his most popular volumes.

KELLY HRUDEY was born at Edmonton, Alberta in 1961 and played major junior hockey for the Medicine Hat Tigers from1978 to 1981. He proceeded to have a stellar two-year Central Hockey League career, being named to the first all-star teams in both 1982 and 1983 and capturing MVP honours winning the Tommy Ivan Trophy in 1983. From1983 until he retired from the NHL in 1998, Kelly Hrudey played in 677 regular season and 85 playoff games recording 271 regular season wins and an additional 36 wins in the playoffs. A second-round pick of the New York Islanders, he played for the East Coast team from 1983 until 1989 before moving west to toil for the Los Angeles Kings (1989-1996) and the San Jose Sharks (1996-1998). More than an excellent athlete, Hrudey has proven himself as an on-air and in-print commentator of the game with *Hockey Night In Canada* and other media outlets. His intelligent and well-spoken presentations have made him a popular and respected voice for the sport especially on his "Behind the Mask" segment on *Hockey Night in Canada*.

GARY HYLAND is a poet, editor, arts activist and former lecturer at University of Regina who lives in Moose Jaw, where he was born in 1940. He taught high school English in Moose Jaw while doing creative writing. His awards include several prizes in the Saskatchewan Writers Guild annual competitions, including major awards for poetry in 1991 and 1995 and the John V. Hicks Award in 2003. Author of numerous poems, Hyland has had several collections of his work published including *Poems from a Loft* (1974), *Home Street* (1975), *Just Off Main* (1982), *Street of Dreams* (1984), *White Crane Spreads Wings* (1996), and *The Work of Snow* (2003). He is currently preparing a new manuscript entitled *You.*

DONNA KANE was born in 1959 and she continues to live in her home town of Dawson Creek, British Columbia. She has attended the Sage Hill Writing Experience in Saskatchewan and the Banff Centre Wired Writing Programme in Alberta. In 2000 she received the Lina Chartrand Award for poetry and she has been co-director of Writing on the Ridge and an active promoter of literary readings and workshops in the Peace River region. Her poetry has appeared in *Descant, Grain, The Fiddlehead,* and *The Malahat Review* as well as in her own collection *Somewhere, a Fire* which was published in 2004. She is currently working on a second collection of poetry.

MICHAEL P.J. KENNEDY, who resides in the Rural Municipality of Vanscoy, Saskatchewan, was born in 1947. He has a B.A. in English with a minor in Education, an M.A. in Anglo-Irish Literature, and a Ph.D. in Canadian Literature. He has taught at University of Ottawa, Concordia University in Montreal, University of Regina, and is currently at University of Saskatchewan and Kelsey Campus of Saskatchewan Institute of Applied Science and Technology where he has taught classes in communication arts, media studies, English, and Canadian Literature. His U. of S. class "Reading Culture: Hockey in Canadian Literature," initiated in 2002, has received national recognition. A freelance sports writer since 1979, he had a college sports column in the Saskatoon *Star Phoenix* for ten years. His publications include hundreds of scholarly, general interest, and sports articles, and those dealing with Inuit Literature, Canadian Studies, railways, and hockey. His *Words on Ice: A Collection of Hockey Prose* appeared in 2003.

JOHN B. LEE was born in 1951 and raised on a farm near Highgate, Ontario. He received an Honours B.A. in English and a B.Ed. and M.A. in teaching English from University of Western Ontario. He has taught high school English, dramatic arts, and creative writing for a decade and has also taught creative writing at Canadore College and University of Windsor. He now makes his living as a full time writer. He was the winner of the Milton Acorn Memorial People's Poetry Award in 1993 and 1995, the Tildon Award for Poetry in 1995, and People's Political Poem winner in 1996. His publications include *In The Terrible Weather of Guns* (2002), *Tongues of the Children* (1996), *The Sign of Perfection: Poems and Stories on the Game of Hockey* (1995), *The Beatles Landed Laughing in New York* (1995), *Variations on Herb* (1993), *These Are the Days of Dogs and Horses* (1994), and *Soldier's Heart* (1998).

J. HUGH MACDONALD, who is retired after thirty-one years of teaching high school, was born in Charlottetown, Prince Edward Island in 1945. He earned a B.A. from St. Dunstan's University (now part of University of Prince Edward Island), and is now a full time writer. His more than twenty books include: *Chung Lee Loves Lobsters* (1992), *Looking for Mother* (1995), *The Digging of Deep Wells* (1997), and *Cold Against the Heart* (2003). He has also co-edited with Brent MacLaine *Landmarks: An Anthology of New Atlantic Poetry of the Land* (2001) and with Alice Reese *A Bountiful Harvest: Fifteen Years of the Island Literary Awards* (2002). He is currently working on *Letting Go; An Anthology of Loss and Survival*. His *Chung Lee Loves Lobsters* won the L.M. Montgomery PEI Literature for Children Award and he was the recipient of the Award for Distinguished Contribution to the Literary Arts on Prince Edward Island in 2004.

FLORENCE MCNEIL born in Vancouver (North Burnaby) in 1937, studied at University of British Columbia with Earle Birney. She received a B.A. and an M.A. in Creative Writing then taught at Western Washington University and University of Calgary. She has published more than ten separate volumes of work since 1967. Eleven books of poetry include *Ghost Towns* (1975), *Barkerville* (1984), *Swiming Out of History: Poems Selected and New* (1991), *A Company of Angels* (1999), and *Slow Twilight of the Standing Stones: The Barra Poems* (2001). Her fiction includes *Miss P. and Me* (1982), *All Kinds of Magic* (1984), and *Breathing Each Others Air* (1994). She has also edited *Do the Whales Jump at Night: An Anthology of Canadian Poetry for Children* (1990).

BRUCE MEYER was born in Toronto in 1957 and received his B.A. and M.A. from University of Toronto and a Ph.D. from McMaster University in Hamilton. He is a professor of English at Laurentian University's Barrie Campus and at St. Michael's College Continuing Education Programme at University of Toronto. He has taught at a number of post-secondary institutions including Trinity College, University of Windsor, McMaster, and Athol Murray College of Notre Dame in Saskatchewan. He is the author of almost two dozen books including *The Golden Thread* (2000), *Oceans* (2004), and *Flights* (2004), and edited a volume of the *Dictionary of Literary Biography* (2003). He has had numerous broadcasts on CBC Radio including the "Great Books" series and his awards include the E.J. Pratt Gold Medal and Prize for Poetry, the Alta Lind Cook Award, and Ruth Cable Memorial Prize. He is currently completing a study of the hero in literature for Harper Collins and a textbook on poetry for Oxford University Press. His latest collection of short fiction, *Flights*, appeared in 2005. A study of his literary works also will appear in the Guernica Writers Series in 2005.

MICHAEL ONDAATJE was born in Ceylon (Sri Lanka) in 1943. He lived in England from 1952 until 1962 when he immigrated to Canada where he attended Bishops University in Quebec and later University of Toronto from which he received his B.A., and Queen's University from which he received his M.A. He has taught at University of Western Ontario and Glendon College of York University. His numerous books of poetry, prose, and his edited anthologies along with his editing of others' work at Coach House Press, *Brick*, and *Quarry* have enabled him to be a major contributor to Canadian Literature. His first book of poetry, *The Dainty Monsters* (1967) was followed by others including a "collage" of poetry and prose *The Collected Works of Billy The Kid* (1970) and novels *Coming Through Slaughter* (1976), *In The Skin of the Lion* (1987), and *The English Patient* (1992). He has won the Governor General's Award in 1971, 1980, 1992, and 2000, the Booker Prize in 1992, and the Giller Prize and Prix Medicis in 2000. He is a member of the Order of Canada.

AL PURDY, who died in 2000, was born at Wooler, Ontario in 1918. Purdy lived and worked at various locations across Canada in the 1930s and this experience plus his military service in the British Columbia interior during World War II was reflected in his poetry. His first book was *The Enchanted Echo* (1944). He won the Governor General's Award for *The Cariboo Horses* in 1965. He published over twenty volumes of poetry winning the Governor General's Award for *The Collected Poems of Al Purdy* (1986) which includes 262 individual poems in 350 pages. Although he did write a novel (*Splinter in the Heart*, 1990) and travel essays as well as book reviews and critical pieces, he is best known for his poetry. Throughout his last decades, he travelled across the country giving readings and was one of the first Canadian authors to support himself as a full time writer. He won the aptly named "People's Poet" Award in 1982 as well as two Governor General's Awards, and the Order of Canada.

THE RHEOSTATICS consist of Dave Bidini (guitar), Tim Vesely (bass), Martin Tielli (lead guitar), and Michael Phillip-Wojewoda (drums, 2004) following Don Kerr (drums) who replaced Dave Clark in 1997. Bidini, Vesely, and Tielli do most of the composition work. The group was formed in the early 1980s in their high school years in the Toronto suburb of Etobicoke. Their albums include *The Rheostatics* (1984), *Canadian Dream* (1986), *Greatest Hits* (1987), *Melville* (1991), *Whale Music* (1992), *Introducing Happiness* (1994), *Music Inspired by the Group of Seven* (1995), *The Blue Hysteria* (1997), *Sweet, Rich, Beautiful, and Mine* (1997), *Double Live* (1998), *The Nightline Session* (1998), *The Story of Harmelodia* (1999), *Night of the Shooting Stars* (2001), *2067* (2004).

KEN RIVARD, who has lived in Calgary since 1976, was born in Montreal in 1947. He holds a Masters degree from McGill University and has worked as a special education teacher at many levels. Currently he spends most of his time writing and teaches one English class at a Calgary college. He has been Writer-in-Residence for The Writers Guild of Alberta and The Calgary Public Library. His publications include two books of poetry: *Kiss Me Down To Size* (1983) and *Frankie's Desires* (1986), short fiction *If She Could Take All These Men* (1995), *Skin Tests* (2000), *Bottle Talk* (2002), *Whiskey Eyes* (2004), and children's literature *Mom The School Flooded* (1996). Current projects include a collection of dramatic monologues and a novel entitled *Mother Wild*.

SIR CHARLES G.D. ROBERTS, along with Bliss Carman, Duncan Campbell Scott, and Archibald Lampman, was one of Canada's "Confederation" poets during the late nineteenth and early twentieth centuries. Born at Douglas, New

Brunswick in 1860, he died in Toronto in 1943. His poetry captured much of the physical beauty of Canada and his animal stories brought a different perspective, that of the animals, to the genre. He published thirteen collections of poetry, nine novels, five novellas, two collections of short fiction, and over 250 individual animal stories. "The Skater" appeared in 1901.

STEPHEN SCRIVER was born at Wolseley, Saskatchewan in 1947, and as a boy assisted his father who edited *The Wolseley News*. After attending university, Scriver taught school at various Saskatchewan communities. In 1974 he discovered creative writing, capturing a W.O. Mitchell Bursary for Saskatchewan School for the Arts at Fort San. In 1977 his first book of hockey poetry, *Between the Lines*, was published. It was followed by the best-selling *All Star Poet!* in 1981 and his third book of hockey poetry, *More All Star Poet!* in 1989. His fourth collection, entitled *Under the Wings*, honoured his father's war service. After moving to Alberta in 1990, Scriver collaborated with Kenneth Brown on the play *Letters in Wartime* which won the Sterling Award for Best New Fringe Work in Edmonton in 1995. His script for the movie *Missing on Way Back* won the Regina Heritage Award. He is currently working on a novel.

JANE SIBERRY was born in Toronto in 1955. She studied piano as a child and received a degree in microbiology from University of Guelph. Her self-titled LP appeared in 1981 followed three years later by *No Borders Here*. In 1985 Siberry released *The Speckless Sky* which went gold and captured two People's Choice Awards in Canada for Album and Producer of the Year. In the years that followed she recorded *The Walking* (1988), *Bound By The Beauty* (1989), *When I Was a Boy* (1993), *Maria* (1995). During the late 1990s she collaborated with others and sang around the world as well as recorded songs for films. In 1996 she started Sheeba Records which featured more releases including *Teenager* (1996), *A Day in the Life* (1997), *Child* (1997), *Lips* (1999), *Tree* (1999), *New York Trilogy* (1999), *Hush* (2000), and *City* (2001). In 2004, Jane Siberry took part in her "Beauty Train Solo Tour" and began writing for an upcoming album *Lily*.

BIRK SPROXTON resides at Red Deer, Alberta where he has taught Canadian Literature and Creative Writing for decades at Red Deer College. Born in Flin Flon, Manitoba in 1943, Sproxton has a B.A. from United College in Winnipeg, and an M.A. and Ph.D. from University of Manitoba. His publications include *Headframe* (1985), *The Hockey Fan Came Riding* (1990), and *The Red-Headed Woman with the Black, Black Heart* which received the Manitoba Historical Society's Award for Historical Fiction. He has also edited *Trace: Prairie Writers on Writing* (1986) and *Great Stories from the Prairies* (2000).

BETSY STRUTHERS, who was born in Toronto in 1951, received her B.A. in English from what was then Waterloo Lutheran University (Wilfred Laurier University) and has held various positions as clerk, promotion manager, and advertising manager at Carleton University in Ottawa, at publishers Peter Martin Associates and Clarke Irwin & Co. in Toronto, and Bata Library at Trent University in Peterborough, Ontario. After being editor of *Canadian Book Review Annual*

(1980), she has been involved with editorial and administrative work for *Journal of Canadian Studies, Alternatives: Journal of Society and the Environment,* Black Moss Press, and Broadview Press. Her poetry books include: *Censored Letters* (1984), *Saying So Out Loud* (1988), *Running Out of Time* (1993), *Virgin Territory* (1996), *Driven* (2000), *Still* (2003), and *In Her Fifties* (2005). She won the Pat Lowther Memorial Award in 2004. Her work appears in numerous anthologies and journals in addition to three collections of her own fiction. *A Studied Death* appeared in 1995, *Grave Deeds* in 1994, and *Found: A Body* in 1992. Her current project is a collection of poems entitled *Second Voice.*

THE TRAGICALLY HIP, originally formed in Kingston, Ontario in 1983, have become one of Canada's most popular groups. The group is comprised of Gordon Downie (lead vocals), Paul Langois (rhythm guitar and backing vocals), Bobby Baker (lead guitar), Gord Sinclair (bass, backing vocals), and Johnny Fay (drums). *EP* appeared in 1987 and was followed by *Up To Here* (1989), *Road Apples* (1991), *Fully Completely* where "Fifty Mission Cap" was recorded (1992), *Day For Night* (1994), *Trouble at the Henhouse* (1996), *Live Between Us* (1997), *Phantom Power* (1998), *Music @ Work* (2000), *In Violet Light* (2002), and *In Between Evolution* (2004).

Hockey in Canadian Literature:
A Selected Bibliography

Compiled by M.P.J.Kennedy, Ph.D.

Alguire, Judith. *Iced*. Norwich, Vermont: New Victoria Publishers, 1995; Toronto: Women's Press, 1995. (novel)

Avery, Joanna and Julie Stevens. *Too Many Men on the Ice: Women's Hockey in North America*. Victoria: Polestar Books, 1997. (non-fiction)

Avison, Margaret. "Thaw." *Always Now: The Collected Poems of Margaret Avison*. Volume 1. Erin, Ontario: Porcupine's Quill, 2003. (poetry)

Batten, Jack. "The Gentle Farmer from Delisle." *Riding on the Roar of the Crowd*. Ed. David Gowdey. Toronto: Macmillan Canada, 1989. 234-249. (non-fiction)

Beardsley, Doug. *Country on Ice*. Winlaw, British Columbia: Polestar, 1987. (non-fiction/autobiography)

Beardsley, Doug. *Our Game: An All-Star Collection of Canadian Hockey Fiction*. Victoria: Polestar Books, 1997. (short fiction)

Beardsley, Doug. *The Rocket, The Flower, The Hammer and Me: An All-Star Collection of Canadian Hockey Fiction*. Winlaw, British Columbia: Polestar Press, 1988. (short fiction)

Beardsley, Doug. "The Sheer Joy of Shinny." *Riding on the Roar of the Crowd*. Ed. David Gowdey. Toronto: Macmillan Canada, 1989. 17-26; *Words on Ice: A Collection of Hockey Prose*. Ed. Michael P.J. Kennedy. Toronto: Key Porter Books, 2003. (non-fiction)

Beddoes, Dick. *Greatest Hockey Stories*. Toronto: Macmillan Canada, 1990. (non-fiction)

Beddoes, Dick. *Hockey: The Story of the World's Fastest Sport*. New expanded edition. New York: Macmillan, 1973. (non-fiction)

Belisle, Dave. *There's a Shark in My Hockey Pool*. Gloucester, Ontario: Self Published, 1998. (fiction)

Benedict, Michael and D'arcy Jenish eds. *Canada on Ice: 50 Years of Great Hockey*. Toronto: Penguin Canada, 1998. (non-fiction)

Berger, Michael et al. *Hockey: The Official Book of the Game*. London: Hamlyn Publishing, 1990. (non-fiction, photographs)

Bidini, Dave. *Tropic of Hockey: My Search for the Game in Unlikely Places*. Toronto: McClelland and Stewart Limited, 2000. (non-fiction)

Book, Rick. "The Game." *Necking with Louise*. New York: Harper Collins (Harper Tempest), 2001. 21-57. (short fiction)

Bowering, George. *Great Canadian Sports Stories*. Ottawa: Oberon Press, 1979. (sports fiction, two hockey stories)

Boyd, Bill. *Hockey Towns: Stories of Small Town Hockey in Canada*. Toronto: Doubleday, 1998; Toronto: Seal Books, 1998. (non-fiction)

Brooks, Kevin and Sean Brooks eds. *Thru the Smoky End Boards: Canadian Poetry about Sports and Games*. Vancouver: Polestar, 1996. (poetry)

Brown, Kenneth. *Alma's Night Out: A Play in One Act*. 1986. *Riding the Roar of the Crowd*. Ed. David Gowdey. Toronto: Macmillan Canada, 1989. 303-318. (drama)

Brown, Kenneth. *Life After Hockey*. Toronto: Playwright's Union of Canada, 1985. (drama)

Brown, Kenneth. *Life After Hockey*. *Five From the Fringe: A Selection of Five Plays First Performed at the Fringe Theatre Event*. Ed. Nancy Bell. Edmonton: NeWest Press, 1986. (drama)

Burnham, Clint. "from Buddyland." *Textual Studies in Canada*. 12 (1998): 50-54. (poetry)

Bushkowsky, Aaron. "The Phantom of Centre of Great Slave Lake." *Grain* (Rural Life Edition). 20.3 (Fall 1992): 235-242; *Words on Ice: A Collection of Hockey Prose*. Ed. Michael P.J. Kennedy. Toronto: Key Porter Books, 2003. 81-89. (short fiction)

Callaghan, Morley. "The Game That Makes a Nation." *Riding on the Roar of the Crowd*. Ed. David Gowdey. Toronto: Macmillan Canada, 1989. 50-52; *Words on Ice: A Collection of Hockey Prose*. Ed. Michael P. J. Kennedy. Toronto: Key Porter Books, 2003. 24-27. (non-fiction)

Carrier, Roch. *La Guerre, Yes Sir!* Trans. Sheila Fischman. Toronto: House of Anansi, 1970. (novel)

Carrier, Roch. *The Hockey Sweater and Other Stories*. Toronto: House of Anansi, 1979; Montreal: Tundra, 1984. (short fiction)

Clausson, Nils. "Breakaway Sonnet." *Ice: New Writing on Hockey*. Ed. Dale Jacobs. Edmonton: Spotted Cow Press, 1999. 159. (poetry)

Connor, Ralph. *Glengarry School Days: A Story of Early Days in Glengarry*. New York: Grosset and Dunlop, 1902. (novel)

Conway, Russ. *Game Misconduct: Alan Eagleson and the Corruption of Hockey*. Toronto: Macfarlane, Walter and Ross, 1995. (non-fiction)

Cosentino, Frank. *The Renfrew Millionaires: The Valley Boys of Winter 1910*. Burnstown, Ontario: General Store Publishing House, 1990. (non-fiction)

Cox, Damien and Gord Stellick. *'67 The Toronto Maple Leafs Their Sensational Victory and the End of an Empire*. Toronto: Wiley and Sons Canada Limited, 2004. (non-fiction)

Crozier, Lorna. "Canadian Angels." *This Morning* CBC Radio One. 21 February 2002. Transcript. 22 February 2002 <http://radio.cbc.ca/insite/THIS_MORNING_TORONTO/2002/2/21> (poetry)

Cruise, David and Alison Griffiths. *Net Worth: Exploding the Myths of Pro Hockey*. Toronto: Viking, 1991. (non-fiction)

Crycob, A., ed. *Xokken/Hockey*. Mockba: 1978. (non-fiction, English/Russian)

Currie, Robert. "Max Bentley and the Hockey Pants." *2000% Cracked Wheat*. Eds. Edna Alford et al. Regina: Coteau Books, 2000. 160-172. (short fiction)

Cuthbert, Chris and Scott Russell. *The Rink: Stories from Hockey's Home Towns*. Toronto: Penguin, 1997. (non-fiction)

Cutler, Michael. *Great Hockey Masks*. Montreal: Tundra, 1983. (non-fiction)

Daniels, Calvin. *Guts and Go: Great Saskatchewan Hockey Stories*. Calgary: Heritage House, 2004. (non-fiction)

Daniels, Calvin. *Skating the Edge*. Saskatoon: Thistledown Press, 2001. (short fiction)

Diamond, Dan. ed. *Total Hockey: The Official Encyclopedia of the National Hockey League*. New York: Total Sports, 1998; 2nd rev. ed. Kingston, New York: Total Sports, 2000. (non-fiction/reference)

Diamond, Dan and James Duplcey. *Hockey Stories on and off the Ice*. Kansas City: Andrews McMeel Publications, 2001. (non-fiction)

Dill, Howard. *Game of Hockey*. 5 February 2002 <http://www.gameofhockey.com> (non-fiction)

Douglas, Thom J. *The Hockey Bibliography*. Toronto: Ontario Institute for Studies in Education, 1978. (non-fiction)

Dowbiggin, Bruce. *Money Players: How Hockey's Greatest Stars Beat the NHL at its Own Game*. Toronto: McClelland and Stewart Limited, 2003. (non-fiction)

Dowbiggin, Bruce. *The Stick: A Celebration, An Elegy*. Toronto: Macfarlane, Walter, and Ross, 2001. (non-fiction)

Dryden, Ken. *The Game: A Thoughtful and Provocative Look at Life in Hockey*. Toronto: Macmillan Canada, 1983, 1993, 1999. Rev. ed. 2003. (non-fiction)

Dryden, Ken and Roy MacGregor. *Home Game: Hockey and Life in Canada*. Toronto: McClelland and Stewart Limited, 1990. (non-fiction)

Dutton, Mervyn "Red," *Hockey: The Fastest Game on Earth*. New York/London: Funk and Wagnells, 1938.

Earle, Neil. "Hockey as Canadian Popular Culture: Team Canada 1972, Television and the Canadian Identity." *Slippery Pastimes Reading the Popular in Canadian Culture*. Eds. Joan Nicks and Jeannette Sloniowski. Waterloo, Ontario: Wilfred Laurier University Press, 2002. 321-343. (non-fiction)

Eckhardt-Smith, Lee Ann. "Playing By The Rules." *Storyteller* (Winter 1999).

Edge, Marc. *Redline, Blueline, Bottomline*. Vancouver: New Star Books, 2004. (non-fiction)

Etue, Elizabeth and Megan K. Williams. *On the Edge: Women Making Hockey History*. Toronto: Second Story Press, 1996. (non-fiction)

Falla, Jack. *Home Ice: Reflections on Backyard Rinks and Frozen Ponds*. Toronto: McClelland and Stewart Limited, 2000. (autobiographical non-fiction essays)

Farrell, Art. *Hockey: Canada's Royal Winter Game*. 1899.

Fawcett, Brian. "My Career With the Leafs." *My Career With the Leafs and Other Stories*. Vancouver: Talonbooks, 1982. 174-190. *Our Game: An All-Star Collection of Hockey Fiction*. Victoria: Polestar, 1997. 180-193. (short fiction)

Fineday, Wes. "The Hockey Game." *Achimoona*. Intro. Maria Campbell. Saskatoon: Fifth House, 1985. 43-49; *Our Game: An All-Star Collection of Hockey Fiction*. Ed. Doug Beardsley. Victoria: Polestar, 1997. 47-51. (short fiction)

Finnigan, Joan. "Grey is the Forelock Now of the Irishman." *A Dream of Lillies*. Frederickton: Fiddlehead Books, 1995. 22-23. (poetry)

Finnigan, Joan. *Old Scores, New Goals: The Story of the Ottawa Senators*. Kingston, Ontario: Quarry Press, 1992. (non-fiction)

Finnigan, Joan. "Rink." *Second Wind, Second Sight*. Windsor, Ontario: Black Moss Press, 1998. 25-27. (poetry)

First, Tina Lincer. "From the Penalty Box: Confessions of a Reluctant Hockey Mom." *Ice: New Writing on Hockey*. Ed. Dale Jacobs. Edmonton: Spotted Cow Press, 1999. 141-150; *Words on Ice: A Collection of Hockey Prose*. Ed. Michael P.J. Kennedy. Toronto: Key-Porter Books, 2003. (non-fiction)

Fischler, Shirley. "The World Hockey Association: Assessing the Impact of the Rival League.'" *Total Hockey*. Ed. Dan Diamond. New York: Total Sports, 1998. 374-375. (non-fiction)

Fischler, Shirley. "A Woman's Game: Nagano Saw It Come of Age, but Women's Hockey has its Own Rich History." *Total Hockey*. Ed. Dan Diamond. New York: Total Sports, 1998. 425-427. (non-fiction)

Fischler, Stan. *Cracked Ice: An Insider's Look at the NHL in Turmoil*. Toronto: McGraw Hill Ryerson, 1995. (non-fiction)

Fischler, Stan and Shirley Fischler, eds. *The Hockey Encyclopedia*. New York: Macmillan, 1983. (non-fiction)

Frayne, Trent, ed. *Trent Frayne's Allstars: An Anthology of Canada's Best Sports Writing*. Toronto: Doubleday Canada, 1996. (non-fiction)

Frayne, Trent and Peter Gzowski. *Great Canadian Sports Stories*. Toronto: Canadian Centennial Publishing Company, 1965. (non-fiction)

Friesen, Gerald. *Hockey, the Prairies and Canada's Cultural History*. Montreal: Misc Publications, 1990. (non-fiction)

Galloway, Steven. *Finnie Walsh*. Vancouver: Raincoast Books, 2000. (novel)

Gaston, Bill. *The Good Body*. Vancouver: Raincoast Books, 2004. (novel)

Gowdey, David, ed. *Riding on the Roar of the Crowd: A Hockey Anthology*. Toronto: Macmillan of Canada, 1989. (non-fiction and short fiction)

Gowdey, David. "Tonight from Make Believe Gardens." *Riding on the Roar of the Crowd*. Ed. David Gowdey. Toronto: Macmillan Canada, 1989. 71-82. (non-fiction)

Gruneau, Richard and David Whitson. *Hockey Night in Canada: Sport, Identities, and Cultural Politics*. Toronto: Garamond Press, 1993. (non-fiction)

Gutteridge, Don. *Bus-Ride*. Ailsa Craig, Ontario: Nairn Publishing House, 1974. (novel)

Gzowski, Peter. *The Game of Our Lives*. Toronto: McClelland and Stewart Limited, 1981; 2nd edition. Introduction by Michael P.J. Kennedy. Surrey, British Columbia: Heritage House, 2004. (non-fiction)

Haliburton, Thomas Chandler. *The Attaché or Sam Slick in England*. London: Richard Bentley, 1844. 112-113. (fiction)

Hall, Ann, et al. *Sport in Canadian Society*. Toronto: McClelland and Stewart Limited, 1991. (non-fiction)

Harrison, Richard. *Hero of the Play*. Toronto: Wolsak and Wynn, 1994. (poetry)

Harrison, Richard. *Hero of the Play: Poems Revised 1994-2004*. Revised 10th Anniversary edition. Foreword by Roy MacGregor. Toronto: Wolsak and Wynn, 2004. (poetry)

Hayes, Don. *The Nature, Incidents, Location, and Causes of Injury in Intercollegiate Ice Hockey.* Springfield, Massachusetts: 1971. (non-fiction)

Hockey's First Ice Age: A Bibliography of Early Hockey Publications (1820-1926). Vancouver: Intreped Publications, 1993. (non-fiction)

Hood, Hugh. *Around the Mountain.* Toronto: Peter Martin Associates, 1967. (short fiction)

Houston, William. *Inside Maple Leaf Gardens: The Rise and Fall of the Toronto Maple Leafs.* Toronto: McGraw Hill Ryerson, 1989. (non-fiction)

Houston, William and David Shoalts. *Eagleson: The Fall of a Hockey Czar.* Toronto: McGraw Hill Ryerson, 1993. (non-fiction)

Howell, Colin D. *Blood, Sweat, and Cheers: Sport and the Making of Modern Canada.* Toronto: University of Toronto Press, 2001. (non-fiction)

Howell, Colin D. *Putting it on Ice: Hockey in Historical and Contemporary Perspective.* Halifax: Gorsebrook Research Institute, St. Mary's University, 2002. (non-fiction)

Hunter, Douglas. *A Breed Apart: An Illustrated History of Goaltenders.* Viking Edition. Toronto: Penguin Books, 1995. (non-fiction)

Hyland, Gary. "The B-P-T." *2000% Cracked Wheat.* Eds. Edna Alford et al. Regina: Coteau Books, 2000. 173-174. (short fiction)

Irvin, Dick. "Writing and Broadcasting." *Total Hockey.* Ed. Dan Diamond. New York: Total Sports, 1998. 116-117. (non-fiction)

Jacobs, Dale, ed. *Ice: New Writing on Hockey a Collection of Poems, Essays, and Short Stories.* Edmonton: Spotted Cow Press, 1999. (poetry, short fiction, essays)

Jarman, Mark Anthony. *Salvage King, Ya! A Herky-Jerky Picaresque.* Vancouver: Anvil Press, 1997. (novel)

Jarman, Mark Anthony. "Righteous Speedboat." *Our Game: An All-Star Collection of Hockey Fiction.* Ed. Doug Beardsley. Victoria: Polestar, 1997. 233-243. (short fiction)

Jenish, D'arcy. *The Stanley Cup: A Hundred Years of Hockey at Its Best.* Toronto: McClelland and Stewart Limited, 1992. (non-fiction)

Johnston, Mike and Ryan Walter. *Simply the Best: Insights and Strategies from Great Hockey Coaches.* Surrey, British Columbia: Heritage House, 2004. (non-fiction)

Johnston, Wayne. *The Divine Ryans.* Toronto: McClelland and Stewart Limited, 1990. (novel)

Jones, Martin. *Hockey's Home: Halifax-Dartmouth The Origin of Canada's Game.* Halifax: Nimbus Publishing, 2002. (non-fiction)

Kane, Donna. "Sudden Death." *Textual Studies in Canada* 12 (1998): 48. (poetry)

Kane, Donna. "Summer Hockey Camp." *Textual Studies in Canada* 12 (1998): 49. (poetry)

Kennedy, Michael P.J. *Going Top Shelf: An Anthology of Canadian Hockey Poetry.* Surrey, British Columbia: Heritage House, 2005 (poetry)

Kennedy, Michael P.J. "Hockey as Metaphor in Selected Canadian Literature." *Textual Studies in Canada* 12 (1998): 81-94. (non-fiction)

Kennedy, Michael P.J. Introduction. *The Game of Our Lives* 2nd ed. by Peter Gzowski. Surrey, British Columbia: Heritage House, 2004. (non-fiction)

Kennedy, Michael P.J. "University Hockey Gaining National Fans." *Saskatoon Sun*. 21 February 1999: B3-4. (non-fiction)

Kennedy, Michael P.J. *Words on Ice: A Collection of Hockey Prose*. Toronto: Key Porter Books, 2003. (short fiction and non-fiction essays)

Kidd, Bruce. *The Struggle for Canadian Sport*. Toronto: University of Toronto Press, 1996. (non-fiction)

Kidd, Bruce and John Macfarlane. *The Death of Hockey*. Toronto: New Press, 1972. (non-fiction)

Kinsella, W.P. "Truth." *The Fencepost Chronicles*. Don Mills, Ontario: Totem Press, 1986. 1-12. *Our Game: An All-Star Collection of Hockey Fiction*. Ed. Doug Beardsley. Victoria: Polestar, 1997. 153-160. (short fiction)

LaSalle, Peter. *Hockey Sur Glace: Stories*. New York: Breakaway Books, 1998. (stories)

Lee, John B. *The Hockey Player Sonnets*. Waterloo, Ontario: Penumbra Press, 1991. (poetry)

Lee, John B. *The Hockey Player Sonnets: Overtime Edition*. Waterloo, Ontario: Penumbra Press, 2003. (poetry)

Lee, John B. *Losers First: Poems and Stories on Game and Sport*. Windsor, Ontario: Black Moss Press, 1999. (poetry and fiction)

Lee, John B., ed. *That Sign of Perfection: From Bandy Legs to Beer Legs, Poems and Stories on the Theme of Hockey*. Windsor: Black Moss Press, 1995. (fiction and poetry)

Ludwig, Jack. *Hockey Night in Moscow*. Toronto: McClelland and Stewart Limited, 1972. (non-fiction)

Ludin, Steve. *When She's Gone*. Winnipeg: Great Plains Publications, 2004. (novel)

MacGregor, Roy. *The Home Team: Fathers, Sons, and Hockey*. Toronto: Penguin, 1995. (non-fiction)

MacGregor, Roy. *The Last Season*. Toronto: Macmillan of Canada, 1983; Toronto: Penguin, 1985. (novel)

MacGregor, Roy. *A Loonie for Luck: A True Fable About Hockey and the Olympics*. Foreword by Wayne Gretzky. Toronto: McClelland and Stewart, 2002. (non-fiction)

MacGregor, Roy. *The Night They Stole the Stanley Cup*. Screech Owls Series. Toronto: McClelland and Stewart Limited, 1995. (juvenile fiction)

MacIntosh, Donald and Donna Greenhorn. "Hockey Diplomacy and Canadian Foreign Policy." *Journal of Canadian Studies*. 28.2 (Summer 1993): 96-112. (non-fiction)

McCormick, Pete. *Understanding Ken*. Vancouver: Douglas and McIntyre, 1998. (novel)

McFarlane, Brian. *One Hundred Years of Hockey*. Toronto: Deneau, 1989. (non-fiction)

McFarlane, Brian. *Proud Past, Bright Future: One Hundred Years of Women's Hockey*. Toronto: Stoddart, 1994. (non-fiction)

McKinley, Michael. *Putting a Roof on Winter: Hockey's Rise from Sport to Spectacle*. Vancouver: Douglas and McIntyre Limited, 2002. (non-fiction)

Manchester, Peter. *50 Things to Make with a Hockey Stick*. Fredericton: Goose Lane, 2002. (non-fiction humour)

Mason, Gary. *On the Road with the Legendary Heroes of Hockey: Old Timers.* Vancouver: Douglas and McIntyre (Greystone Books), 2002. (non-fiction)

Mildon, Marsha. "Number 33." *Our Game: An All-Star Collection of Hockey Fiction.* Ed. Doug Beardsley. Victoria: Polestar Book Publishers, 1997. 200-209; *Words on Ice: A Collection of Hockey Prose.* Ed. Michael P.J. Kennedy. Toronto: Key Porter Books, 2003. 197-207. (short fiction)

Moffet, Gilles. "Toronto Maple Leafs Goaltending History." *Goalies' World.* 3 (May/June 1996): 22-23. (non-fiction)

Morrison, John and Doug McClatchy. *Toronto Blue Shirts.* Stouffville, Ontario: Hockey Information Service, 1996. (non-fiction)

Morrison, Scott. *The Days Canada Stood Still: Canada vs U.S.S.R.* Toronto: McGraw Hill, 1989. (non-fiction)

Morrison, Scott. "The Rise and Fall of R. Alan Eagleson." *Total Hockey.* Ed. Dan Diamond. New York: Total Sports, 1998. 118-120. (non-fiction)

National Hockey League. *Official Guide and Record Book: 2005.* Toronto: National Hockey League, 2004. (non-fiction)

Nielson, Robert. *Athlete's Foot: or How I Failed at Sports.* Watertown, Ontario: Potlatch Publications Limited, 2002. (non-fiction)

Novak, Michael. *The Joy of Sports: End Zones, Bases, Baskets, Balls, and Consecration of the American Sport.* New York: Basic, 1976. (non-fiction)

O'Brien, Andy. *The Jacques Plante Story.* Toronto: McGraw-Hill Ryerson, 1972. (biography)

Olver, Robert. *The Making of Champions: Life in Canada's Junior A Leagues.* Markham, Ontario: Penguin Canada, 1990. (non-fiction)

Ondaatje, Michael. "To A Sad Daughter." *An Anthology of Canadian Literature in English.* Rev. and Abridged Ed. Russell Brown et al. Toronto: Oxford University Press, 1990; *A New Anthology of Canadian Literature in English.* Eds. Donna Bennet and Russell Brown. Don Mills, Ontario: Oxford University Press, 2002. 894-895. (poetry)

Orr, Frank. *Puck is a Four Lettered Word.* Toronto: Methuen, 1982. (novel)

Paci, F.G. *Icelands.* Ottawa: Oberon Press, 1999. (novel)

Percival, Lloyd. *The Hockey Handbook.* 1951. Rev. Ed. Toronto: Copp Clark, 1957. (non-fiction)

Plante, Jacques. *On Goaltending.* Montreal: Robert Davies Multimedia Publications, 1997. (non-fiction)

Plante, Jacques. *Step By Step Hockey Goaltending.* Montreal: Studio 9 Books, 1997. (non-fiction)

Plante, Raymond. *Jacques Plante: Behind the Mask.* Lantzville, British Columbia: XYZ Press, 2001. (biography)

Plimpton, George. *Open Net.* New York: W.W. Norton, 1985. (non-fiction)

Podnieks, Andrew. *Lord Stanley's Cup.* Bolton, Ontario: Fenn Publishing Company, 2004. (non-fiction)

Podnieks, Andrew, et al. eds. *Kings of the Ice: A History of World Hockey.* Richmond Hill, Ontario: NDE Publishing, 2002. (non-fiction)

Purdy, Al. "Hockey Players." *The Collected Poems of Al Purdy.* Ed. Russell Brown. Toronto: McClelland and Stewart Limited, 1986. 54-56. (poetry)

Purdy, Al. "The Time of Your Life." *The Collected Poems of Al Purdy.* Ed. Russell Brown. Toronto: McClelland and Stewart Limited, 1986. 192-194. (poetry)

Quarrington, Paul. *King Leary*. 1987. Seal Books. Toronto: McClelland and Stewart-Bantam Limited, 1988. (novel)

Quarrington, Paul. *Logan in Overtime*. Toronto: Doubleday Canada, 1990. (novel)

Reddick, Don. *Dawson City Seven*. Fredericton: Goose Lane Editions, 1993. (novel)

Richards, David Adams. *Hockey Dreams: Memories of a Man Who Couldn't Play*. 1996. Toronto: Anchor Canada, 2001. (autobiography)

Richler, Mordecai. "Cheap Skates." *Dispatches from the Sporting Life*. Guilford, Connecticut: The Lyons Press, 2002. 141-148. (non-fiction)

Robertson, Ray. *Heroes*. Toronto: Dundurn Group, 2000. (novel)

Roche, (Wilfred Victor) Bill. *The Hockey Book: The Great Hockey Stories of All Time*. Toronto: McClelland and Stewart, 1953. (non-fiction)

Roxborough, Henry. *One Hundred-Not Out: The Story of Nineteenth Century Canadian Sport*. Toronto: Ryerson Press, 1966. (non-fiction)

Salutin, Rick. *Les Canadiens*. Vancouver: Talonbooks, 1977. (drama)

Scanlan, Lawrence. *Grace Under Fire: The State of Our Sweet and Savage Game*. Toronto: Penguin Canada, 2002. (non-fiction)

Scanlan, Wayne. *Roger's World: the Life and Unusual Times of Roger Neilson*. Toronto: McClelland and Stewart Limited, 2004. (non-fiction)

Schomperlen, Diane. *Hockey Night in Canada: Stories by Diane Schomperlen*. Kingston: Quarry Press, 1987. (short fiction)

Scriver, Stephen. *All Star Poet!* Moose Jaw: Coteau Books, 1981. (poetry)

Scriver, Stephen. *Between The Lines*. Saskatoon: Thistledown Press, 1977. (poetry)

Scriver, Stephen. *More All Star Poet: New and Selected Poems*. Regina: Coteau Books, 1989. (poetry)

Shea, Kevin. *Barilko: Without a Trace*. Bolton, Ontario: Fenn Publishing Company, 2004. (non-fiction)

Shikaze, Steven. "Hockey Dreams." *Ice: New Writing on Hockey*. Ed. Dale Jacobs. Edmonton: Spotted Cow Press, 1999. 202-205. (Short fiction)

Shinny: The Hockey in All of Us. Dir. David Battistella. National Film Board of Canada, 2001. (non-fiction documentary)

Shostak, Peter. *Hockey...Under Winter Skies*. Victoria: Yalenka Enterprises, 2000. (autobiographical anecdotes/drawings)

Silver, Jim. *Thin Ice: Money, Politics, and the Demise of an NHL Franchise*. Halifax: Fernwood Publishing, 1996. (non-fiction)

Sinden, Harry. *Hockey Showdown: The Canada Russia Hockey Series*. Toronto: Doubleday Canada, 1972. (non-fiction)

Smythe, Conn with Scott Young. *If You Can't Beat 'Em in the Alley*. Toronto: McClelland and Stewart Limited, 1981. (non-fiction)

Sproxton, Birk. *The Hockey Fan Came Riding*. Red Deer: Red Deer College Press, 1990. (autobiography/fiction/poetry)

Sproxton, Birk. "The Hockey Fan Goes Reading." *The Hockey Fan Goes Riding*. Red Deer: Red Deer College Press, 1990. 109. (autobiography)

Sproxton, Birk. "The Hockey Fan Reflects on Beginnings." *The Hockey Fan Came Riding*. Red Deer: Red Deer College Press, 1990. 29-30. (autobiography/ fiction/poetry)

Sproxton, Birk. "Hockey is a Transition Game." *The Hockey Fan Came Riding.* Red Deer: Red Deer College Press, 1990. 25. (non-fiction)

Sproxton, Birk. "A Point About Style." *The Hockey Fan Came Riding.* Red Deer: Red Deer College Press, 1990. 31. (non-fiction/grammar)

Sproxton, Birk. "Replay." *The Hockey Fan Came Riding.* Red Deer: Red Deer College Press, 1990. 32-35. (autobiography/fiction/ poetry)

Sproxton, Birk. "The Song of the Stay-at-Home Defenceman." *The Hockey Fan Came Riding.* Red Deer: Red Deer College Press, 1990. 50-52. (autobiography/fiction/poetry)

Sproxton, Birk. "A Stich in Time." *The Hockey Fan Came Riding.* Red Deer: Red Deer College Press, 1990. 59-60. (autobiography/fiction/poetry)

Sproxton, Birk. "What the Coach Said." *The Hockey Fan Came Riding.* Red Deer: Red Deer College Press, 1990. 53-55. (found poetry)

Stenson, Fred. "Colourful." *Textual Studies in Canada: Canada's Journal of Cultural Literacy* 12 (1998): 69-79. (short fiction)

Stenson, Fred. *Teeth.* Regina: Coteau Press, 1994. (short stories)

Stewart, Barbara. *She Shoots...She Scores! A Complete Guide to Girl's and Women's Hockey.* Toronto: Doubleday Canada, 1998. (non-fiction)

Stewart, Mark. *Hockey: A History of the Fastest Game on Ice.* New York: Franklin Watts, 1998. (non-fiction)

Surgent, Scott Adam. "Cause and Effect: The Birth of the World Hockey Association." *The Complete Historical and Statistical Reference to the World Hockey Association 1972-1979.* Ed. Scott Adam Surgent. Tempe, Arizona: Xaler Press, 1995. 7-9. (non-fiction)

Sylvester, Kevin. *Shadrin has Scored for Russia! The Day Canadian Hockey Died A Mockumentary.* Toronto: Stoddard Publishing, 2001. (fiction)

Thauberger, Rudy. "Goalie." *Our Game: An All-Star Collection of Hockey Fiction.* Ed. Doug Beardsley. Victoria: Polestar, 1997. 213-217. (short fiction)

Theberger, Nancy. *Higher Goals: Women's Ice Hockey and the Politics of Gender.* Albany, New York: State University of New York, 2000. (non-fiction)

Theberger, Nancy. "It's Part of the Game: Physicality and the Production of Gender in Women's Hockey." *Gender and Society* 11.1 (1971): 61-87. (non-fiction)

Theberger, Nancy. "Playing with the Boys: Manon Rhéaume, Women's Hockey, and the Struggle for Legitimacy." *Canadian Women's Studies Journal.* 15.4 (Fall 1995): 37-41. (non-fiction)

Turowetz, Alan and Chrys Goyens. *Lions in Winter.* Scarborough, Ontario: Prentice-Hall Canada, 1986; Markham, Ontario: Penguin Books, 1987; Toronto: McGraw-Hill Ryerson, 1994. (non-fiction)

Ursell, Geoffrey. "Last Minute of Play." *100% Cracked Wheat.* Eds. Bob Currie, et al. Moose Jaw: Coteau Books, 1983. 57-58. (poetry)

Urstadt, Bryant. *The Greatest Hockey Stories Ever Told: The Finest Writers on Ice.* Guilford, Connecticut: Lyons Press, 2004. (U.S. fiction/non-fiction)

Valgardson, W.D. "The Hockey Fan." *The Hockey Fan.* Victoria: Hawthorne Society, 1994. (short fiction)

van Belkom, Edo. "Hockey's Night in Canada." *Ice: New Writing on Hockey.* Ed. Dale Jacobs. Edmonton: Spotted Cow Press, 1999. 70-81. (short fiction)

Vaughan, Garth. "Ice Hockey in Nova Scotia: From Hurley to Hockey on Frozen Ponds." *Total Hockey: The Official Encyclopedia of the National Hockey League.* Ed. Dan Diamond. New York: Total Sports, 1998. 3-6. (non-fiction)

Vaughan, Garth. *The Puck Stops Here: The Origin of Canada's Great Winter Game.* Fredericton: Goose Lane Editions, 1996. (non-fiction)

Wagamese, Richard. *Keeper'n Me.* 1994. Toronto: Doubleday Canada, 1996. (novel)

Walsh, Mary. Dir. Jackie Maxwell. *Hockey Wives.* Toronto: Factory Theatre Laboratory Archives, 1988. (drama)

Walsh, Mary. *Hockey Wives.* Toronto: Toronto Free Theatre Archives, unproduced reading script, 1980. (drama)

Wheeler, Jordan. "SAP." *Voices: Being Native in Canada.* Eds. Linda Jaine and Drew Hayden Taylor. Saskatoon: University of Saskatchewan Extension Division, 1992. 170-179. (short fiction)

Willes, Ed. *The Rebel League: The Short and Unruly Life of the World Hockey Association.* Toronto: McClelland and Stewart Limited, 2004. (non-fiction)

Wimmer, Dick. *Fastest Game: An Anthology of Hockey Writings.* Indianapolis: Masters Press, 1997. (non-fiction)

Wright, Richard B. *The Age of Longing.* Toronto: Harper Collins, 1995; 1st HarperPerennial Canada edition. Toronto: HarperPerennial, 2001. (novel)

Young, Scott. *The Boys of Saturday Night: Inside Hockey Night in Canada.* Toronto: Macmillan Canada, 1990. (non-fiction)

Young, Scott. *Hello Canada: The Life and Times of Foster Hewitt.* Toronto: Seal, 1985. (non-fiction)

Zeman, Brenda. *88 Years of Puck-Chasing in Saskatchewan.* Regina: Saskatchewan Sports Hall of Fame, 1983. (non-fiction)

Zeman, Gary. *Alberta on Ice.* Edmonton: Westweb Press, 1985. (non-fiction)

Zweig, Eric. *Hockey Night in the Dominion of Canada.* Toronto: Lester Publishing, 1992. (historical novel)

More Hockey Books
from Heritage House

The Game of Our Lives
Peter Gzowski

This best-selling hockey classic tells the incredible story of the Edmonton Oilers'
1980–81 season when the team was poised on the edge of greatness.
"This is a classic of hockey writing." *The Globe and Mail*

978-1-894384-59-6

Simply the Best: Insights and Strategies from Great Hockey Coaches
Mike Johnston and Ryan Walter

Simply the Best delivers rare insights on success straight from the hearts and minds of
winning coaches including Scotty Bowman, Marc Crawford, Jacques Demers, Ken
Hitchcock, Pat Quinn, and Mike Keenan. Recognized as the greatest coaches in the
game, these "elite 12" openly discuss in their own words strategies that have made
them successful.

978-1-894974-37-0

Simply the Best: Players on Performance
Mike Johnston and Ryan Walter

What makes players simply the best? That's what coach Mike Johnston and former
NHL great Ryan Walter set out to discover in *Simply the Best: Players on Performance*.
The authors interviewed Sidney Crosby, Cassie Campbell, Shane Doan, Jarome Iginla,
Ed Jovanovski, Trevor Linden, Scott Niedermayer, Joe Sakic and Hayley Wickenheiser
to discover how they prepare to be the best in the world, how they lead a dressing
room from the inside out, and how coaches best inspire their winning performances.

978-1-894974-24-0

Guts and Go Overtime: More Great Saskatchewan Hockey Stories
Calvin Daniels

Whether it's a great event like the Moosomin Moose playing marathon hockey to set
a Guinness World Record and raise money for a new town hospital or the exciting
play of Shaunavon's Rhett Warrener of the Calgary Flames, readers will discover that
Guts and Go Overtime is written for anyone, young or old, who enjoys hockey and
good stories, regardless of where they live.

978-1-894974-02-8

Ask for these great books at your local bookstore,
or visit www.heritagehouse.ca